Machine Learning

A Simple, Concise & Complete Introduction to Machine Learning for Beginners (Contains 2 Texts: Machine Learning for Beginners and Machine Learning for Absolute Beginners)

Machine Learning for Beginners

The Definitive Guide to Neural Networks, Random Forests, and Decision Trees

the information in question by the reader will render any resulting actions solely under their purview. There are no scenarios in which the publisher or the original author of this work can be in any fashion deemed liable for any hardship or damages that may befall them after undertaking information described herein.

Additionally, the information found on the following pages is intended for informational purposes only and should thus be considered, universal. As befitting its nature, the information presented is without assurance regarding its continued validity or interim quality. Trademarks that are mentioned are done without written consent and can in no way be considered an endorsement from the trademark holder.

Table of Contents

Introduction

Thank you for downloading Machine Learning for Beginners: *The Definitive Guide to Neural Networks, Random Forests, and Decision Trees*, and thank you for doing so. Research is continuously going on in several pet projects around universities and research centers across the world on Machine Learning. In more detail, there are different programming languages like Java, which are used in training Neural Networks. Using several languages, one can visualize all that is going on in the Neural Networks and play around with different hyper-parameter settings.

There is a growing number of people who are seeking to understand neural networks and what powers them up. To that end, the following chapters are going to discuss the algorithmic functions, methods, and code that make Neural Networks work well. You are going to follow codes that are being used to create algorithmic functions that are best used in random forests. Furthermore, you are going to see how neural networks make decisions using decision trees. This is to present algorithms in ways that will make you start out your journey in this field.

You might be tempted to jump right to the end to learn about Neural networks, but before you get there, forget about getting to learn everything at once, and focus on getting the principles that are in every chapter, so that you can gain an understanding of how the whole structure works.

There are very many books that are available in the market that explain this concept in detail, and thanks again for choosing this book. Every effort was applied to ensure that this book is useful in the understanding of the Neural network, decision trees, and random forests.

Chapter 1: MNIST Classification by the Use of Logistic Regression

We are going to start by looking at Theano or Python.

Tips on Theano

When experimenting, it is possible to engage in it for hours or even days. After the exercise, the gradient-descent can take the time to identify the appropriate parameters. Once you have determined the weights, you will need to save them, together with the estimates you will be getting, when the search continues.

Pickle is the best option if you want to save the parameters for your models. For instance, if you have shared variables, a, b, c, you will save the command like shown below:

```
>>> import cPickle
>>> save_file = open('path', 'wb')   # this will overwrite
>>> cPickle.dump(w.get_value(borrow=True), save_file, -1)
>>> cPickle.dump(v.get_value(borrow=True), save_file, -1)
>>> cPickle.dump(u.get_value(borrow=True), save_file, -1)
>>> save_file.close()
```

The data can be loaded later on like below

```
>>> save_file = open('path')
>>> w.set_value(cPickle.load(save_file), borrow=True)
>>> v.set_value(cPickle.load(save_file), borrow=True)
>>> u.set_value(cPickle.load(save_file), borrow=True)
```

This is a verbose technique which has been tried and tested. You don't need to worry because your data will be loaded and rendered in matplotlib easily, even when the aliens decide to invade earth.

No need to train functions for long term archiving

Pickle mechanisms and Python's deep-copy are compatible with Theano functions, even though the use of pickle in Theano functions should not be done. In case an update on the Theano folder is done, and any other change is done in the internal elements, then you will have a hard time to unpickle the model. Theano is on its development period, and there are expected changes in the internal APIs. If you want to be safe, your training should not be pickled in its entirety for long term storage, because it is ideal for short term storing. An example is the temp file or a copy that is made during a job distribution.

Intermediate Results plotting

To understand your models, a powerful way to interpret it is using visualizations. An insertion of PIL commands for image rendering, or plotting commands in matplotlib can be tempting. This is placed in the training script. If by any chance you see something interesting later on, on the pre-rendered images, and you find something that is not clear, you will be inclined to investigate it. By then, you will be chasing smoking mirrors because you will wish that you had saved the work.

If you have space on your hard disk, the intermediate models should be saved by the training script, and the saved models should process the visualization script.

If you are keen enough, you will notice that you have a model-saving function, and this is what you will use to save intermediate models. Consider learning more about the matplotlib, PIL which is the Python Image Library.

Now, we will show more on how Theano can implement a common classifier called the logistic regression. We will have a preview on the model's primer which is a refresher and an anchorage of the notation, and also a way to showcase the mathematical expressions on Theano graphs.

In deep ML(Machine Learning), MNIST classification problem is tackled.

The Model

A common linear classifier is the logistic-regression. The weight matrix W and a vector bias b parameterize the probabilistic classifier. An input vector is projected to a hyperplane set in order to achieve classification. Remember that each hyperplane and a particular class are directly related. The distance between the input and the hyperplanes reflects the potential that the input has in relation to a particular class.

The Theano code to be used is as follows

```
# initialize with 0 the weights W as a matrix of shape (n_in, n_out)
self.W = theano.shared(
    value=numpy.zeros(
        (n_in, n_out),
        dtype=theano.config.floatX
    ),
    name='W',
    borrow=True
)
# initialize the biases b as a vector of n_out 0s
self.b = theano.shared(
    value=numpy.zeros(
        (n_out,),
        dtype=theano.config.floatX
    ),
    name='b',
    borrow=True
)

# symbolic expression for computing the matrix of class-membership
# probabilities
# Where:
# W is a matrix where column-k represent the separation hyperplane for
# class-k
# x is a matrix where row-j  represents input training sample-j
# b is a vector where element-k represent the free parameter of
# hyperplane-k
self.p_y_given_x = T.nnet.softmax(T.dot(input, self.W) + self.b)

# symbolic description of how to compute prediction as class whose
# probability is maximal
self.y_pred = T.argmax(self.p_y_given_x, axis=1)
```

The parameters of the model have to be consistent through the entire training session; therefore, variables that are shared are allocated to W and b. This is a declaration of both variables as Theano variables that are symbolic, but the contents are also initialized. The calculation of vector $P(Y |x, W, b)$, the Softmax operator and the dot are used. The vector-types symbolic variable is produced as p_y_given_x.

Use the T.argmax operator to find the model's actual prediction. This operator is then used to return an index that is maximal at p_y_given_x.

The code we have written does not save the world or do anything just yet; it's just a code. This is because its operators are at the initial state. We are going to learn optimal parameters.

Loss function definition

While studying optimal parameters, a loss function is an important subject to consider. In multi-class logistic-progression, negative log representation is common to be used as the loss. This is similar to likelihood maximization. It is the same as maximizing the data set D likelihood under a parameterized o for the model.

$$\mathcal{L}(\theta = \{W, b\}, \mathcal{D}) = \sum_{i=0}^{|\mathcal{D}|} \log(P(Y = y^{(i)} | x^{(i)}, W, b))$$

$$\ell(\theta = \{W, b\}, \mathcal{D}) = -\mathcal{L}(\theta = \{W, b\}, \mathcal{D})$$

The gradient descent is a simple method that is used for minimizing nonlinear functions, compared to the more popular minimization. We are going to use stochastic gradient-method using mini-batches. Below is a Theano code that shows a minibatch loss.

```python
class LogisticRegression(object):
    """Multi-class Logistic Regression Class

    The logistic regression is fully described by a weight matrix :math:`W`
    and bias vector :math:`b`. Classification is done by projecting data
    points onto a set of hyperplanes, the distance to which is used to
    determine a class membership probability.
    """

    def __init__(self, input, n_in, n_out):
        """ Initialize the parameters of the logistic regression

        :type input: theano.tensor.TensorType
        :param input: symbolic variable that describes the input of the


                      architecture (one minibatch)

        :type n_in: int
        :param n_in: number of input units, the dimension of the space in
                     which the datapoints lie

        :type n_out: int
        :param n_out: number of output units, the dimension of the space in
                      which the labels lie

        """
        # start-snippet-1
        # initialize with 0 the weights W as a matrix of shape (n_in, n_out)
        self.W = theano.shared(
            value=numpy.zeros(
                (n_in, n_out),
                dtype=theano.config.floatX
            ),
            name='W',
            borrow=True
        )
        # initialize the biases b as a vector of n_out 0s
        self.b = theano.shared(
            value=numpy.zeros(
                (n_out,),
                dtype=theano.config.floatX
            ),
            name='b',
            borrow=True
        )

        # symbolic expression for computing the matrix of class-membership
        # probabilities
        # Where:
        # W is a matrix where column-k represent the separation hyperplane for
        # class-k
        # x is a matrix where row-j  represents input training sample-j
        # b is a vector where element-k represent the free parameter of
        # hyperplane-k
        self.p_y_given_x = T.nnet.softmax(T.dot(input, self.W) + self.b)
```

```python
        # symbolic description of how to compute prediction as class whose
        # probability is maximal
        self.y_pred = T.argmax(self.p_y_given_x, axis=1)
        # end-snippet-1

        # parameters of the model
        self.params = [self.W, self.b]

        # keep track of model input
        self.input = input

    def negative_log_likelihood(self, y):


        """Return the mean of the negative log-likelihood of the prediction
        of this model under a given target distribution.

        .. math::

            \frac{1}{|\mathcal{D}|} \mathcal{L} (\theta=\{W,b\}, \mathcal{D}) =
            \frac{1}{|\mathcal{D}|} \sum_{i=0}^{|\mathcal{D}|}
                \log(P(Y=y^{(i)}|x^{(i)}, W,b)) \\
            \ell (\theta=\{W,b\}, \mathcal{D})

        :type y: theano.tensor.TensorType
        :param y: corresponds to a vector that gives for each example the
                  correct label

        Note: we use the mean instead of the sum so that
              the learning rate is less dependent on the batch size
        """
        # start-snippet-2
        # y.shape[0] is (symbolically) the number of rows in y, i.e.,
        # number of examples (call it n) in the minibatch
        # T.arange(y.shape[0]) is a symbolic vector which will contain
        # [0,1,2,... n-1] T.log(self.p_y_given_x) is a matrix of
        # Log-Probabilities (call it LP) with one row per example and
        # one column per class LP[T.arange(y.shape[0]),y] is a vector
        # v containing [LP[0,y[0]], LP[1,y[1]], LP[2,y[2]], ...,
        # LP[n-1,y[n-1]]] and T.mean(LP[T.arange(y.shape[0]),y]) is
        # the mean (across minibatch examples) of the elements in v,
        # i.e., the mean log-likelihood across the minibatch.
        return -T.mean(T.log(self.p_y_given_x)[T.arange(y.shape[0]), y])
        # end-snippet-2

    def errors(self, y):
        """Return a float representing the number of errors in the minibatch
        over the total number of examples of the minibatch ; zero one
        loss over the size of the minibatch
```

```python
def errors(self, y):
    """Return a float representing the number of errors in the minibatch
    over the total number of examples of the minibatch ; zero one
    loss over the size of the minibatch

    :type y: theano.tensor.TensorType
    :param y: corresponds to a vector that gives for each example the
              correct label
    """

    # check if y has same dimension of y_pred
    if y.ndim != self.y_pred.ndim:
        raise TypeError(
            'y should have the same shape as self.y_pred',
            ('y', y.type, 'y_pred', self.y_pred.type)
        )
    # check if y is of the correct datatype
    if y.dtype.startswith('int'):
        # the T.neq operator returns a vector of 0s and 1s, where 1
        # represents a mistake in prediction
        return T.mean(T.neq(self.y_pred, y))
    else:
```

Chapter 2: Multi-Layer Perception (MLP)

This is the next architecture that is presented by Theano. A Multi-Layer Perception can also be identified like a classifier in logistic regression; this is because there is a transformation of the input that is transformed by the use of a learned nonlinear transformation. There is a projection of the input data to a space using transformation projects, which makes it become separable linearly. The hidden layer is what is used to describe an intermediate layer. MLPs can be **universal approximators** by the use of one hidden layer.

The Model

The diagram below shows one layer hidden neural network.

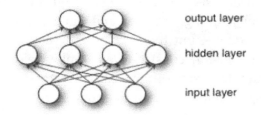

output layer

hidden layer

input layer

Ideally, a layer of hidden is represented by a function $f: R^D \to R^L$, where D is the same as the x vector, in size. L's the same as vector output $f(x)$, because, when you look at the matrix notation,

$$f(x) = G(b^{(2)} + W^{(2)}(s(b^{(1)} + W^{(1)}x))),$$

Has $b^{(1)}$ and $b^{(2)}$ as bias vectors; matrices as weight $W^{(1)}$, $W^{(2)}$ then G and s *as* activation functions.

Vector $h(x) = \Phi(x) = s(b^{(1)} + W^{(1)}x)$ has a layer that is hidden

$$W^{(1)} \in R^{D \times D_h}$$
.

This represents a weight matrix that is connected to both the hidden layer and the input vector. Every single column $W^{(1)}_{\cdot i}$ is a representation of the weights that go to the i-th unit that is hidden, from the input units. The choices that are available for *s* include *tanh, with* $tanh(a)=(e^a-e^{-a})/(e^a+e^{-a})$, or the *sigmoid* function, that has $sigmoid(a)=1/(1+e^{-a})$. Tanh will be used since it yields better local maxima and faster training. Sigmoid and Tanh are scalar-to-scalar functions, but the tensors and vectors in their natural extension consist when applied elementary. For instance, separating each vectors element, achieving a vector that is of the same size.

Then, $o(x) = G(b^{(2)} + W^{(2)}h(x))$ is the vectors output. Keep in mind that the form used in MNIST classification digits using Logistic Regression in chapter 1. Obtaining of class membership probabilities is possible using G which is the *Softmax* function.

In MLP training, all model parameters are learned, and SGD (Stoch-Gradient Descent) is used with mini batches. The set $\theta = \{W^{(2)}, b^{(2)}, W^{(1)}, b^{(1)}\}$ is the one that is used in learning. Backpropagation algorithm can be obtained through. The good thing is that Theano does differentiation automatically.

Heading to MPL from logistic regression

We are going to focus on MLP hidden layer. A class representation of a hidden layer is started. To have the MLP constructed, there has to be a layer of logistic regression at the top.

```
class HiddenLayer(object):
    def __init__(self, rng, input, n_in, n_out, W=None, b=None,
                 activation=T.tanh):
```

"""

An MLP hidden layer: fully-connected units and have activation functions for sigmoid. W Weight matrix having the shape (n_out, n_in,)
and b which is the bias vector of (n_out,) shape.
NOTE: The nonlinearity used here is tanh
tanh(dot(input,W) + b) provides the activation that is hidden

: type rng: numpy.random.RandomState

: param rng: a generator that produces random numbers that initialize weights

: type input: theano.tensor.dmatrix

: param input: a symbolic tensor of shape (n_examples, n_in)

: type n_in: int

: param n_in: dimensionality of input

: type n_out: int

: param n_out: no. of units that are hidden

: type activation: theano.Op or function

: param activation: hidden layer to use Nonlinearity
"""

self.input = input

The initial weights value of the hidden layer needs to be sampled uniformly from an interval that is dependent and symmetric on the activation function. Initialization makes certain that when training is in progress, every single neuron function that is in its activation function allows propagation of information in both upwards and downwards direction. When we talk about upwards, we mean that there is a flow of activation from the input to the output. On the contrary, a backward propagation means that the gradient flows from the output to the inputs.

Theoretically, the graph is implemented by the graph that calculates the value of the hidden layer $h(x) = \Phi(x) = s(b^{(1)} + W^{(1)}x)$. If this graph is used in the *Logistic Regression class* as an input, it is then implemented in the MNIST classification logistic

Regression, as the MLP becomes the output. The following MLP class short implementation is described below.

```python
class MLP(object):
    """Multi-Layer Perceptron Class

    A multilayer perceptron is a feedforward artificial neural network model
    that has one layer or more of hidden units and nonlinear activations.
    Intermediate layers usually have as activation function tanh or the
    sigmoid function (defined here by a ``HiddenLayer`` class) while the
    top layer is a softmax layer (defined here by a ``LogisticRegression``
    class).
    """

    def __init__(self, rng, input, n_in, n_hidden, n_out):
        """Initialize the parameters for the multilayer perceptron

        :type rng: numpy.random.RandomState
        :param rng: a random number generator used to initialize weights

        :type input: theano.tensor.TensorType
        :param input: symbolic variable that describes the input of the
        architecture (one minibatch)

        :type n_in: int
        :param n_in: number of input units, the dimension of the space in
        which the datapoints lie

        :type n_hidden: int
        :param n_hidden: number of hidden units

        :type n_out: int
        :param n_out: number of output units, the dimension of the space in
        which the labels lie

        """

        # Since we are dealing with a one hidden layer MLP, this will translate
        # into a HiddenLayer with a tanh activation function connected to the
        # LogisticRegression layer; the activation function can be replaced by
        # sigmoid or any other nonlinear function
        self.hiddenLayer = HiddenLayer(
            rng=rng,
            input=input,
            n_in=n_in,


            n_out=n_hidden,
            activation=T.tanh
        )

        # The logistic regression layer gets as input the hidden units
        # of the hidden layer
        self.logRegressionLayer = LogisticRegression(
            input=self.hiddenLayer.output,
            n_in=n_hidden,
            n_out=n_out
        )
```

21

We are also going to use regularization of L1 and L2, and we are also going to calculate the norm L1 and the norm L2 of $W^{(1)}$, $W^{(2)}$.

```
# L1 norm ; one regularization option is to enforce L1 norm to
# be small
self.L1 = (
    abs(self.hiddenLayer.W).sum()
    + abs(self.logRegressionLayer.W).sum()
)

# square of L2 norm ; one regularization option is to enforce
# square of L2 norm to be small
self.L2_sqr = (
    (self.hiddenLayer.W ** 2).sum()
    + (self.logRegressionLayer.W ** 2).sum()
)

# negative log likelihood of the MLP is given by the negative
# log likelihood of the output of the model, computed in the
# logistic regression layer
self.negative_log_likelihood = (
    self.logRegressionLayer.negative_log_likelihood
)
# same holds for the function computing the number of errors
self.errors = self.logRegressionLayer.errors

# the parameters of the model are the parameters of the two layer it is
# made out of
self.params = self.hiddenLayer.params + self.logRegressionLayer.params
```

The model is then trained by the use of stochastic-gradient-descent with the help of mini-batches. The main difference comes in cost function modification so that there is the inclusion of regularization. L1_reg and L2_REG control the terms of regularization in the function of the total cost. The new cost code is as below:

```
# the cost we minimize during training is the negative log likelihood of
# the model plus the regularization terms (L1 and L2); cost is expressed
# here symbolically
cost = (
    classifier.negative_log_likelihood(y)
    + L1_reg * classifier.L1
```

The gradient is then used to update the model. The code comes close to imitate the logistic regression's code, with the number of parameters causing the difference. In order to hack this difference, we are going to be like Superman, use our super strength to pull the two worlds together. Well, that's a wild wish; what we are going to do, is to write a code that will allow any number of parameters to work. Using the parameters list that we developed earlier, and parse the params model, and then compute each steps gradient.

```
# compute the gradient of cost with respect to theta (sotred in params)
# the resulting gradients will be stored in a list gparams
gparams = [T.grad(cost, param) for param in classifier.params]

# specify how to update the parameters of the model as a list of
# (variable, update expression) pairs

# given two lists of the same length, A = [a1, a2, a3, a4] and
# B = [b1, b2, b3, b4], zip generates a list C of same size, where each
# element is a pair formed from the two lists :
#     C = [(a1, b1), (a2, b2), (a3, b3), (a4, b4)]
updates = [
    (param, param - learning_rate * gparam)
    for param, gparam in zip(classifier.params, gparams)
]

# compiling a Theano function 'train_model' that returns the cost, but
# in the same time updates the parameter of the model based on the rules
# defined in 'updates'
train_model = theano.function(
    inputs=[index],
    outputs=cost,
    updates=updates,
    givens={
        x: train_set_x[index * batch_size: (index + 1) * batch_size],
        y: train_set_y[index * batch_size: (index + 1) * batch_size]
    }
)
```

Condensation of the points

We have looked into the basic concepts that can help one to easily write an MLP. We are going to look at how this is done, in a way that is analogous to the implementation of the logistic regression seen previously.

```
"""
This tutorial introduces the multilayer perceptron using Theano.

 A multilayer perceptron is a logistic regressor where
instead of feeding the input to the logistic regression you insert a
intermediate layer, called the hidden layer, that has a nonlinear
activation function (usually tanh or sigmoid) . One can use many such
hidden layers making the architecture deep. The tutorial will also tackle
the problem of MNIST digit classification.




 .. math::

     f(x) = G( b^{(2)} + W^{(2)}( s( b^{(1)} + W^{(1)} x))),

 References:

     - textbooks: "Pattern Recognition and Machine Learning" -
                 Christopher M. Bishop, section 5

"""
__docformat__ = 'restructedtext en'


import os
import sys
import timeit

import numpy

import theano
import theano.tensor as T


from logistic_sgd import LogisticRegression, load_data


# start-snippet-1
class HiddenLayer(object):
    def __init__(self, rng, input, n_in, n_out, W=None, b=None,
                 activation=T.tanh):
        """
        Typical hidden layer of a MLP: units are fully-connected and have
        sigmoidal activation function. Weight matrix W is of shape (n_in, n_o
        and the bias vector b is of shape (n_out,).

        NOTE : The nonlinearity used here is tanh

        Hidden unit activation is given by: tanh(dot(input, W) + b)

        :type rng: numpy.random.RandomState
        :param rng: a random number generator used to initialize weights

        :type input: theano.tensor.dmatrix
        :param input: a symbolic tensor of shape (n_examples, n_in)

        :type n_in: int
        :param n_in: dimensionality of input

        :type n_out: int
        :param n_out: number of hidden units

        :type activation: theano.Op or function
        :param activation: Non linearity to be applied in the hidden
```

24

```
                        layer
        """
        self.input = input
        # end-snippet-1

        # 'W' is initialized with 'W_values' which is uniformly sampled
        # from sqrt(-6./(n_in+n_hidden)) and sqrt(6./(n_in+n_hidden))
        # for tanh activation function
        # the output of uniform if converted using asarray to dtype
        # theano.config.floatX so that the code is runable on GPU
        # Note : optimal initialization of weights is dependent on the
        #        activation function used (among other things).
        #        For example, results presented in [Xavier10] suggest that you
        #        should use 4 times larger initial weights for sigmoid
        #        compared to tanh
        #        We have no info for other function, so we use the same as
        #        tanh.
        if W is None:
            W_values = numpy.asarray(
                rng.uniform(
                    low=-numpy.sqrt(6. / (n_in + n_out)),
                    high=numpy.sqrt(6. / (n_in + n_out)),
                    size=(n_in, n_out)
                ),
                dtype=theano.config.floatX
            )
            if activation == theano.tensor.nnet.sigmoid:
                W_values *= 4

            W = theano.shared(value=W_values, name='W', borrow=True)

        if b is None:
            b_values = numpy.zeros((n_out,), dtype=theano.config.floatX)
            b = theano.shared(value=b_values, name='b', borrow=True)

        self.W = W
        self.b = b

        lin_output = T.dot(input, self.W) + self.b
        self.output = (
            lin_output if activation is None
            else activation(lin_output)
        )
        # parameters of the model
        self.params = [self.W, self.b]


# start-snippet-2
class MLP(object):
    """Multi-Layer Perceptron Class

    A multilayer perceptron is a feedforward artificial neural network model
    that has one layer or more of hidden units and nonlinear activations.
```

Intermediate layers usually have as activation function tanh or the sigmoid function (defined here by a ``HiddenLayer'' class)  while the top layer is a softmax layer (defined here by a ``LogisticRegression'' class).
***

```python
def __init__(self, rng, input, n_in, n_hidden, n_out):
    """Initialize the parameters for the multilayer perceptron

    :type rng: numpy.random.RandomState
    :param rng: a random number generator used to initialize weights

    :type input: theano.tensor.TensorType
    :param input: symbolic variable that describes the input of the
    architecture (one minibatch)

    :type n_in: int
    :param n_in: number of input units, the dimension of the space in
    which the datapoints lie

    :type n_hidden: int
    :param n_hidden: number of hidden units

    :type n_out: int
    :param n_out: number of output units, the dimension of the space in
    which the labels lie

    """

    # Since we are dealing with a one hidden layer MLP, this will translat
    # into a HiddenLayer with a tanh activation function connected to the
    # LogisticRegression layer; the activation function can be replaced by
    # sigmoid or any other nonlinear function
    self.hiddenLayer = HiddenLayer(
        rng=rng,
        input=input,
        n_in=n_in,
        n_out=n_hidden,
        activation=T.tanh
    )

    # The logistic regression layer gets as input the hidden units
    # of the hidden layer
    self.logRegressionLayer = LogisticRegression(
        input=self.hiddenLayer.output,
        n_in=n_hidden,
        n_out=n_out
    )
    # end-snippet-2 start-snippet-3
    # L1 norm ; one regularization option is to enforce L1 norm to
    # be small
    self.L1 = (
        abs(self.hiddenLayer.W).sum()
```

```
    + abs(self.logRegressionLayer.W).sum()
)

# square of L2 norm ; one regularization option is to enforce
# square of L2 norm to be small
self.L2_sqr = (
    (self.hiddenLayer.W ** 2).sum()
    + (self.logRegressionLayer.W ** 2).sum()
)

# negative log likelihood of the MLP is given by the negative
# log likelihood of the output of the model, computed in the
# logistic regression layer
self.negative_log_likelihood = (
    self.logRegressionLayer.negative_log_likelihood
)
# same holds for the function computing the number of errors
self.errors = self.logRegressionLayer.errors

# the parameters of the model are the parameters of the two layer it is
# made out of
self.params = self.hiddenLayer.params + self.logRegressionLayer.params
# end-snippet-3

# keep track of model input
self.input = input


def test_mlp(learning_rate=0.01, L1_reg=0.00, L2_reg=0.0001, n_epochs=1000,
             dataset='mnist.pkl.gz', batch_size=20, n_hidden=500):
    """
    Demonstrate stochastic gradient descent optimization for a multilayer
    perceptron

    This is demonstrated on MNIST.

    :type learning_rate: float
    :param learning_rate: learning rate used (factor for the stochastic
    gradient

    :type L1_reg: float
    :param L1_reg: L1-norm's weight when added to the cost (see
    regularization)

    :type L2_reg: float
    :param L2_reg: L2-norm's weight when added to the cost (see
    regularization)

    :type n_epochs: int
    :param n_epochs: maximal number of epochs to run the optimizer

    :type dataset: string
    :param dataset: the path of the MNIST dataset file from
```

```
    http://www.iro.umontreal.ca/~lisa/deep/data/mnist/mnist.pkl.gz

"""
datasets = load_data(dataset)

train_set_x, train_set_y = datasets[0]
valid_set_x, valid_set_y = datasets[1]
test_set_x, test_set_y = datasets[2]

# compute number of minibatches for training, validation and testing
n_train_batches = train_set_x.get_value(borrow=True).shape[0] / batch_size
n_valid_batches = valid_set_x.get_value(borrow=True).shape[0] / batch_size
n_test_batches = test_set_x.get_value(borrow=True).shape[0] / batch_size

#########################
# BUILD ACTUAL MODEL #
#########################
print '... building the model'

# allocate symbolic variables for the data
index = T.lscalar()  # index to a [mini]batch
x = T.matrix('x')  # the data is presented as rasterized images
y = T.ivector('y')  # the labels are presented as 1D vector of
                     # [int] labels

rng = numpy.random.RandomState(1234)

# construct the MLP class
classifier = MLP(
    rng=rng,
    input=x,
    n_in=28 * 28,
    n_hidden=n_hidden,
    n_out=10
)

# start-snippet-4
# the cost we minimize during training is the negative log likelihood of
# the model plus the regularization terms (L1 and L2); cost is expressed
# here symbolically
cost = (
    classifier.negative_log_likelihood(y)
    + L1_reg * classifier.L1
    + L2_reg * classifier.L2_sqr
)
# end-snippet-4

# compiling a Theano function that computes the mistakes that are made
# by the model on a minibatch
test_model = theano.function(
    inputs=[index],
    outputs=classifier.errors(y),
```

```
    givens={
        x: test_set_x[index * batch_size:(index + 1) * batch_size],
        y: test_set_y[index * batch_size:(index + 1) * batch_size]
    }
)

validate_model = theano.function(
    inputs=[index],
    outputs=classifier.errors(y),
    givens={
        x: valid_set_x[index * batch_size:(index + 1) * batch_size],
        y: valid_set_y[index * batch_size:(index + 1) * batch_size]
    }
)

# start-snippet-5
# compute the gradient of cost with respect to theta (sotred in params)
# the resulting gradients will be stored in a list gparams
gparams = [T.grad(cost, param) for param in classifier.params]

# specify how to update the parameters of the model as a list of
# (variable, update expression) pairs

# given two lists of the same length, A = [a1, a2, a3, a4] and
# B = [b1, b2, b3, b4], zip generates a list C of same size, where each
# element is a pair formed from the two lists :
#    C = [(a1, b1), (a2, b2), (a3, b3), (a4, b4)]
updates = [
    (param, param - learning_rate * gparam)
    for param, gparam in zip(classifier.params, gparams)
]

# compiling a Theano function `train_model` that returns the cost, but
# in the same time updates the parameter of the model based on the rules
# defined in `updates`
train_model = theano.function(
    inputs=[index],
    outputs=cost,
    updates=updates,
    givens={
        x: train_set_x[index * batch_size: (index + 1) * batch_size],
        y: train_set_y[index * batch_size: (index + 1) * batch_size]
    }
)
# end-snippet-5

###############
# TRAIN MODEL #
###############
print '... training'

# early-stopping parameters
patience = 10000  # look as this many examples regardless
```

```python
patience_increase = 2  # wait this much longer when a new best is
                       # found
improvement_threshold = 0.995  # a relative improvement of this much is
                               # considered significant
validation_frequency = min(n_train_batches, patience / 2)
                               # go through this many
                               # minibatche before checking the network
                               # on the validation set; in this case we
                               # check every epoch

best_validation_loss = numpy.inf
best_iter = 0
test_score = 0.
start_time = timeit.default_timer()

epoch = 0
done_looping = False

while (epoch < n_epochs) and (not done_looping):
    epoch = epoch + 1
    for minibatch_index in xrange(n_train_batches):

        minibatch_avg_cost = train_model(minibatch_index)
        # iteration number
        iter = (epoch - 1) * n_train_batches + minibatch_index

        if (iter + 1) % validation_frequency == 0:
            # compute zero-one loss on validation set
            validation_losses = [validate_model(i) for i
                                 in xrange(n_valid_batches)]
            this_validation_loss = numpy.mean(validation_losses)

            print(
                'epoch %i, minibatch %i/%i, validation error %f %%' %
                (
                    epoch,
                    minibatch_index + 1,
                    n_train_batches,
                    this_validation_loss * 100.
                )
            )

            # if we got the best validation score until now
            if this_validation_loss < best_validation_loss:
                #improve patience if loss improvement is good enough
                if (
                    this_validation_loss < best_validation_loss *
                    improvement_threshold
                ):
                    patience = max(patience, iter * patience_increase)

                best_validation_loss = this_validation_loss
                best_iter = iter
```

```
# test it on the test set
test_losses = [test_model(i) for i
                    in xrange(n_test_batches)]
test_score = numpy.mean(test_losses)

print(('     epoch %i, minibatch %i/%i, test error of '
       'best model %f %%') %
      (epoch, minibatch_index + 1, n_train_batches,
       test_score * 100.))

        if patience <= iter:
            done_looping = True
            break

end_time = timeit.default_timer()
print(('Optimization complete. Best validation score of %f %% '
       'obtained at iteration %i, with test performance %f %%') %
      (best_validation_loss * 100., best_iter + 1, test_score * 100.))
print >> sys.stderr, ('The code for file ' +
                      os.path.split(__file__)[1] +
                      ' ran for %.2fm' % ((end_time - start_time) / 60.))


if __name__ == '__main__':
    test_mlp()
```

The user can then run the code by calling :

```
python code/mlp.py
```

The output one should expect is of the form :

```
Optimization complete. Best validation score of 1.690000 % obtained at iteration 2070000,
The code for file mlp.py ran for 97.34m
```

On an Intel(R) Core(TM) i7-2600K CPU @ 3.40GHz the code runs with approximately 10.3 epoch/minute and it took 828 epochs to reach a test error of 1.65%.

Chapter 3: Convolutional Neural Networks

This chapter can be understood well after the first two chapters have been read. We are going to use new functions of Theano and the concepts: shared Variables, downsample, T.grad, conv2d floatX, dimshuffle and basic arithmetic ops. A good GPU is needed to run this, with at least a 1GB RAM. If you have connected your monitor to the GPU, then you may need a bigger RAM size. This is because, if the GPU is hooked to your monitor, each GPU function call will take some seconds as a limit when calling a function in the GPU. If this limit would not be present, you will witness a lot of screen hanging or freezing for a long time. But if you have not connected your GPU to the monitor, then you won't have any time limit. If you experience a timeout issue, you will only lower the size of the batch and you are good to go.

Motivation

One Neural Network variant of the MLP that is referred to as Convolutional is inspired biologically. In a study of the neural cortex of a cat, it was discovered that the visual cortex has an intricate cells arrangement. The cells are very sensitive to minute sub-regions of the visual field that is referred to as a receptive field. The whole visual field is covered and the cells represent local filters that are designed to take advantage of the natural images local correlation.

There are types of cells which have been discovered; the cells types in question are what we call complex and simple cells.

Simple: they are responsive to edge-like-patterns that are in their receptive fields.

Complex: these cells have a larger field of reception which are invariant to the patterns definite position. The most powerful visual cortex is the animal visual cortex. This is because it has an amazing processing system, which is the best example to learn from. This has made many models of neural networks to be designed in the literature. Some of the most common inspired-models are LeNET-5, HMAX, and Neocognitron.

Sparse Connectivity

CNN's enforce a local connectivity pattern between layers that are adjacent and neurons, to exploit the spatially-local-correlation. This means that the hidden input units in the m layer originate from unit subsets of layer $m-1$ that possess receptive fields that are spatially contiguous. To view it graphically, check out the diagram below:

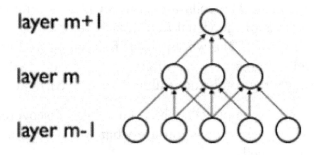

layer m+1

layer m

layer m-1

Consider layer m-1 being the input of retina. Using the figure above, **m's** layer input has fields that are receptive. These fields have width three in the input of the retina, and they are linked to three neurons that are located adjacent to each other in the retina. Layer m+1 units have the same kind of connection as the one below. Their receptive-field has 3 concerning the layer that follows. But if you look at the receptive field compared to the input, it's larger. Outside the field of reception, the units are not responsive to variations that are related with the retina. The learned filters are taken care of by the architecture to produce strong responses to an input pattern that is local.

Like it has been seen above, the stacking of layers like this makes it ideal for filters that become global. For instance, the hidden layers **m+1** units can encode a nonlinear 5 width pixel space.

Shared Weights

Each filter in CNN is duplicated across the whole visual field. These units that have been duplicated have similar parameterization, forming a *feature map*.

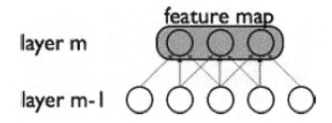

In the figure above, there are three units that are hidden that belong to one feature map. The same weights have the same color. Shared parameters can be learned by the gradient descent, with a minute change to the algorithm. The gradients sum of the parameters is what is called the shared weight's gradient. CNNs are enabled to get better vision generalization by the use of constraints.

Details and Notation

A repeated application of the sub-regions functions of the whole image obtains a feature map. This means that the input image convolution uses a linear filter, adds a bias term and applies a nonlinear-function. If k-th in a feature map is denoted at a selected given layer as h^k, and the filters are done by weights W^k, and b_k bias, then h^k, which is the feature map is obtained using:

$$h_{ij}^k = \tanh((W^k * x)_{ij} + b_k).$$

To have a more detailed data representation, several feature maps are in every hidden layer, $\{h^{(k)}, k=0..K\}$. Each hidden layer Weights W can be represented in a containing element of a 4D-tensor. This is for each collection of the following maps (source-feature and destination-feature) together with source positions, horizontal and vertical. Using a vector that has an element for each destination-feature-map, there can be a representation of the biases b. Graphically, we can represent this as below:

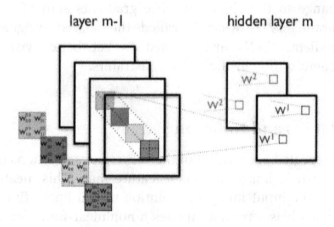

This is a representation of two VNN layers. We have Layer **m-1** which has 4 feature maps. Then we have the Hidden-layer **m** which has 2 feature maps (h^1 and h^0). The neuron outputs that are in h^1 and h^0, that are visible in red and blue squares, are calculated from the layer **m-1** that is in their 2x2 receptive field. You should take note of how the receptive field covers the feature map inputs. Weights W^0 & W^1 of h^0 and h^1 are tensors of 3D weight. The input feature-maps are indexed by the leading dimension, while the pixel coordinates are referred to the other two.

When you summarize it all, W^{kl}_{ij} represents each pixel's weight connection of the maps k-th feature when you look at the m layer, while having the coordinates of the pixel at (i,j) on the layer(m-1) of the 1-th feature map.

Convolution Operator

The main workhorse is the ConvOp that is used to implement Theanos convolutional layer. ConvOp is utilized by theano.tensor.signal.conv2d that takes 2 inputs that are symbolic. There are two inputs that are taken by these, which are:

- A 4D tensor that corresponds to input images that are mini batch. The tensors shape is identified by [image height, mini-batch size, image width, no. of feature input maps]

- A 4D tensor that corresponds to weight matrix W. The tensors shape is: [no. of feature maps that are at layer m, filter width, filter height, no. of features at layer m-1]

Let us look at the Theano code that implements a convolutional layer. There are 3-feature maps that are

of 120x160 size. 2 convolutional filters that have 9x9 receptive fields are used.

```python
import theano
from theano import tensor as T
from theano.tensor.nnet import conv

import numpy

rng = numpy.random.RandomState(23455)

# instantiate 4D tensor for input
input = T.tensor4(name='input')

# initialize shared variable for weights.
w_shp = (2, 3, 9, 9)
w_bound = numpy.sqrt(3 * 9 * 9)
W = theano.shared( numpy.asarray(
            rng.uniform(
                low=-1.0 / w_bound,
                high=1.0 / w_bound,
                size=w_shp),
            dtype=input.dtype), name ='W')

# initialize shared variable for bias (1D tensor) with random values
# IMPORTANT: biases are usually initialized to zero. However in this
# particular application, we simply apply the convolutional layer to
# an image without learning the parameters. We therefore initialize
# them to random values to "simulate" learning.
b_shp = (2,)
b = theano.shared(numpy.asarray(
            rng.uniform(low=-.5, high=.5, size=b_shp),
            dtype=input.dtype), name ='b')
```

```
# build symbolic expression that computes the convolution of input wit
conv_out = conv.conv2d(input, W)

# build symbolic expression to add bias and apply activation function.
# A few words on ''dimshuffle'' :
#    ''dimshuffle'' is a powerful tool in reshaping a tensor;
#    what it allows you to do is to shuffle dimension around
#    but also to insert new ones along which the tensor will be
#    broadcastable;
#    dimshuffle('x', 2, 'x', 0, 1)
#    This will work on 3d tensors with no broadcastable
#    dimensions. The first dimension will be broadcastable,
#    then we will have the third dimension of the input tensor as
#    the second of the resulting tensor, etc. If the tensor has
#    shape (20, 30, 40), the resulting tensor will have dimensions
#    (1, 40, 1, 20, 30). (AxBxC tensor is mapped to 1xCx1xAxB tensor)
#    More examples:
#     dimshuffle('x') -> make a 0d (scalar) into a 1d vector
#     dimshuffle(0, 1) -> identity
#     dimshuffle(1, 0) -> inverts the first and second dimensions
#     dimshuffle('x', 0) -> make a row out of a 1d vector (N to 1xN)
#     dimshuffle(0, 'x') -> make a column out of a 1d vector (N to Nx1)
#     dimshuffle(2, 0, 1) -> AxBxC to CxAxB
#     dimshuffle(0, 'x', 1) -> AxB to Ax1xB
#     dimshuffle(1, 'x', 0) -> AxB to Bx1xA
output = T.nnet.sigmoid(conv_out + b.dimshuffle('x', 0, 'x', 'x'))

# create theano function to compute filtered images
f = theano.function([input], output)
```

Let's dig in and have some fun

```
import numpy
import pylab
from PIL import Image

# open random image of dimensions 639x516
img = Image.open(open('doc/images/3wolfmoon.jpg'))
# dimensions are (height, width, channel)
img = numpy.asarray(img, dtype='float64') / 256.

# put image in 4D tensor of shape (1, 3, height, width)
img_ = img.transpose(2, 0, 1).reshape(1, 3, 639, 516)
filtered_img = f(img_)

# plot original image and first and second components of output
pylab.subplot(1, 3, 1); pylab.axis('off'); pylab.imshow(img)
pylab.gray();
# recall that the convOp output (filtered image) is actually a "minibatch",
# of size 1 here, so we take index 0 in the first dimension:

pylab.subplot(1, 3, 2); pylab.axis('off');
pylab.imshow(filtered_img[0, 0, :, :])
pylab.subplot(1, 3, 3); pylab.axis('off');
pylab.imshow(filtered_img[0, 1, :, :])
pylab.show()
```

Below is the expected generated output

You should notice that a random initialized filter is the one that behaves like edge detectors. The same weight initialization formula has been used with MLP. There is a random sampling of the weights from a distribution that is uniform, which ranges from [-1/fan-in, to 1/fan-in]. Here, fan-in represents the unit-inputs that are hidden. In Multi-Layer Perceptions, it looks into the layer below and represents the units in it. When you go to CNN, you need to consider the input features, together with the size of the receptive field.

Max Pooling

Max Pooling is one important concept in CNN that is a nonlinear form of down-sampling. Max pooling segments input images to rectangular non-overlapping sets, and when you look at each sub-region, the max value is yielded as an output.

Vision benefits from max-pooling because of 2 simple reasons

- It eliminates values that are non-maximal, reducing upper layer computation.

- A translation invariance is provided. Think about cascading a max pool layer using a convolution layer; it's a sight for sore eyes. One can translate input images in eight different directions using just one pixel. When max pooling is implemented on a 2x2 region, three of the eight configurations that are possible produce the same convolutional layer output. When max pooling goes to 3x3, it jumps to 5/8.

- Since additional robustness is provided, max pooling is an efficient way of reducing intermediate representations dimensionality.

- Max-pooling in Theano is done by theano.tensor.signal.downsample.max_pool_2d/ an N dimensional tensor is taken as an input. It is also taken as a downscaling factor that does max pooling over the 2 trailing tensor dimensions.

You might have gotten lost in the explanation, but not to worry. If you understand coding much more, then here is your pie!

```
from theano.tensor.signal import downsample

input = T.dtensor4('input')
maxpool_shape = (2, 2)
pool_out = downsample.max_pool_2d(input, maxpool_shape,

ignore_border=True)

f = theano.function([input],pool_out)

invals = numpy.random.RandomState(1).rand(3, 2, 5, 5)
```

```
print 'With ignore_border set to True:'
print 'invals[0, 0, :, :] =\n', invals[0, 0, :, :]
print 'output[0, 0, :, :] =\n', f(invals)[0, 0, :, :]

pool_out = downsample.max_pool_2d(input, maxpool_shape,
```

ignore_border=False)

```
f = theano.function([input],pool_out)
print 'With ignore_border set to False:'
print 'invals[1, 0, :, :] =\n ', invals[1, 0, :, :]
print 'output[1, 0, :, :] =\n ', f(invals)[1, 0, :, :]
```

The following output should be generated:

```
With ignore_border set to True:
    invals[0, 0, :, :] =
    [[  4.17022005e-01    7.20324493e-01    1.14374817e-04
     [  9.23385948e-02    1.86260211e-01    3.45560727e-01
     [  4.19194514e-01    6.85219500e-01    2.04452250e-01
     [  6.70467510e-01    4.17304802e-01    5.58689828e-01
     [  8.00744569e-01    9.68261576e-01    3.13424178e-01
```

```
3.02332573e-01 1.46755891e-01]
3.96767474e-01 5.38816734e-01]
8.78117436e-01 2.73875932e-02]
1.40386939e-01 1.98101489e-01]
6.92322616e-01 8.76389152e-01]]
```

```
output[0, 0, :, :] =
[[ 0.72032449  0.39676747]
 [ 0.6852195   0.87811744]]
```

```
With ignore_border set to False:
    invals[1, 0, :, :] =
    [[ 0.01936696  0.67883553  0.21162812  0.26554666  0.49157316]
     [ 0.05336255  0.57411761  0.14672857  0.58930554  0.69975836]
     [ 0.10233443  0.41405599  0.69440016  0.41417927  0.04995346]
     [ 0.53589641  0.66379465  0.51488911  0.94459476  0.58655504]
     [ 0.90340192  0.1374747   0.13927635  0.80739129  0.39767684]]
    output[1, 0, :, :] =
    [[ 0.67883553  0.58930554  0.69975836]
     [ 0.66379465  0.94459476  0.58655504]
     [ 0.90340192  0.80739129  0.39767684]]
```

If you compare it to most codes of Theano, the max_pool_2d is special. The downscaling factor is required, represented by *ds* which will be known in the graph building. This changes as we carry on.

LeNet: The Full Model

Convolutional layers, Sparse, and max-pooling are usually central in LeNet models. The modular details vary; you can use the diagram below to see the pictorial representation of the LeNet model.

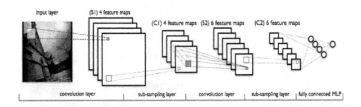

Max-pooling and convolution are what constitutes the lower layers. A traditional MLP which comprises of the logistic regression and the hidden layer is what the upper layer corresponds and fully connects to. The layer below that has all the feature maps has the input set to the 1st fully connected layer.

When you look at the implementation perspective, layers that are on the low work on tensors that are 4D. A 2 Dimensional matrix is achieved after the 4-dimensional matrix is flattened, forming feature maps that are rasterized, and that are compatible to the MLP that was previously implemented.

Summary by combining it all

A LeNet model is now easy to implement since we have all we need. To start us off, we use the LeNetConvPoolLayer class that implements the max-pool and convolution layer.

```
class LeNetConvPoolLayer(object):
    """Pool Layer of a convolutional network """

    def __init__(self, rng, input, filter_shape, image_shape,

                    poolsize=(2, 2)):

    Allocate a LeNetConvPoolLayer with shared variable internal parameters.
    :type rng: numpy.random.RandomState
    :param rng: a random number generator used to initialize weights

    :type input: theano.tensor.dtensor4
    :param input: symbolic image tensor, of shape image_shape

    :type filter_shape: tuple or list of length 4
    :param filter_shape: (number of filters, num input feature maps,
                         filter height, filter width)

    :type image_shape: tuple or list of length 4
    :param image_shape: (batch size, num input feature maps,
                        image height, image width)

    :type poolsize: tuple or list of length 2
    :param poolsize: the downsampling (pooling) factor (#rows, #cols)
    """
```

```
assert image_shape[1] == filter_shape[1]
self.input = input

# there are "num input feature maps * filter height * filter width"
# inputs to each hidden unit
fan_in = numpy.prod(filter_shape[1:])
# each unit in the lower layer receives a gradient from:
# "num output feature maps * filter height * filter width" /
#   pooling size
fan_out = (filter_shape[0] * numpy.prod(filter_shape[2:]) /
           numpy.prod(poolsize))
# initialize weights with random weights
W_bound = numpy.sqrt(6. / (fan_in + fan_out))
self.W = theano.shared(
    numpy.asarray(
        rng.uniform(low=-W_bound, high=W_bound, size=filter_shape),
        dtype=theano.config.floatX
    ),
    borrow=True
)

# the bias is a 1D tensor -- one bias per output feature map
b_values = numpy.zeros((filter_shape[0],), dtype=theano.config.floatX)
self.b = theano.shared(value=b_values, borrow=True)

# convolve input feature maps with filters
conv_out = conv.conv2d(
    input=input,
    filters=self.W,
    filter_shape=filter_shape,
    image_shape=image_shape
)

# downsample each feature map individually, using maxpooling
pooled_out = downsample.max_pool_2d(
    input=conv_out,
    ds=poolsize,
    ignore_border=True
)
```

When initializing the weight values, the no. of feature maps, input and the receptive field's size determine the fan-in. In closing, the Logistic Regression class that is defined in MNIST Classification digits and the Hidden Layer class that is defined in Multilayer Perception can be instantiated in the network as follows.

```python
x = T.matrix('x')    # the data is presented as rasterized images
y = T.ivector('y')   # the labels are presented as 1D vector of
                     # [int] labels


######################
# BUILD ACTUAL MODEL #
######################
print '... building the model'

# Reshape matrix of rasterized images of shape (batch_size, 28 * 28)
# to a 4D tensor, compatible with our LeNetConvPoolLayer
# (28, 28) is the size of MNIST images.
layer0_input = x.reshape((batch_size, 1, 28, 28))

# Construct the first convolutional pooling layer:
# filtering reduces the image size to (28-5+1 , 28-5+1) = (24, 24)
# maxpooling reduces this further to (24/2, 24/2) = (12, 12)
# 4D output tensor is thus of shape (batch_size, nkerns[0], 12, 12)
layer0 = LeNetConvPoolLayer(
    rng,
    input=layer0_input,
    image_shape=(batch_size, 1, 28, 28),
    filter_shape=(nkerns[0], 1, 5, 5),
    poolsize=(2, 2)
)

# Construct the second convolutional pooling layer
# filtering reduces the image size to (12-5+1, 12-5+1) = (8, 8)
# maxpooling reduces this further to (8/2, 8/2) = (4, 4)
# 4D output tensor is thus of shape (batch_size, nkerns[1], 4, 4)
layer1 = LeNetConvPoolLayer(
    rng,
    input=layer0.output,
    image_shape=(batch_size, nkerns[0], 12, 12),
    filter_shape=(nkerns[1], nkerns[0], 5, 5),
```

```
    poolsize=(2, 2)
)

# the HiddenLayer being fully-connected, it operates on 2D matrices of
# shape (batch_size, num_pixels) (i.e matrix of rasterized images).
# This will generate a matrix of shape (batch_size, nkerns[1] * 4 * 4),
# or (500, 50 * 4 * 4) = (500, 800) with the default values.
layer2_input = layer1.output.flatten(2)

# construct a fully-connected sigmoidal layer
layer2 = HiddenLayer(
    rng,
    input=layer2_input,
    n_in=nkerns[1] * 4 * 4,
    n_out=500,
    activation=T.tanh
)

# classify the values of the fully-connected sigmoidal layer
layer3 = LogisticRegression(input=layer2.output, n_in=500, n_out=10)

# the cost we minimize during training is the NLL of the model
cost = layer3.negative_log_likelihood(y)

# create a function to compute the mistakes that are made by the model
test_model = theano.function(
    [index],
    layer3.errors(y),
    givens={
        x: test_set_x[index * batch_size: (index + 1) * batch_size],
        y: test_set_y[index * batch_size: (index + 1) * batch_size]
    }
)

validate_model = theano.function(
    [index],
    layer3.errors(y),
    givens={
        x: valid_set_x[index * batch_size: (index + 1) * batch_size],
        y: valid_set_y[index * batch_size: (index + 1) * batch_size]
    }
)

# create a list of all model parameters to be fit by gradient descent
params = layer3.params + layer2.params + layer1.params + layer0.params

# create a list of gradients for all model parameters
grads = T.grad(cost, params)

# train_model is a function that updates the model parameters by
# SGD Since this model has many parameters, it would be tedious to
# manually create an update rule for each model parameter. We thus
# create the updates list by automatically looping over all
```

47

```
# (params[i], grads[i]) pairs.
updates = [
    (param_i, param_i - learning_rate * grad_i)
    for param_i, grad_i in zip(params, grads)
]

train_model = theano.function(
    [index],
    cost,
    updates=updates,
    givens={
        x: train_set_x[index * batch_size: (index + 1) * batch_size],
        y: train_set_y[index * batch_size: (index + 1) * batch_size]
    }
)
```

Since the code that does all the early stopping and the training is similar to the MLP, it is left out. The code can then be called:

python code/convolutional_mlp.py

Some of the output that you should see include

```
Optimization complete.
Best validation score of 0.910000 % obtained at

iteration 17800,with test


performance 0.920000 %
The code for file convolutional_mlp.py ran for 380.28m
```

Chapter 4: Classes of Learning Algorithms

We are now going to learn about the learning algorithms like linear methods, neural networks, nearest neighbor methods and support vector machines.

Linear Methods

It is one of the oldest supervised ML algorithms in statistics. The main assumption is on the variable output Y, which is of H. The variable Y is a description of the collection of linear variables that are used as input, they are, X1,....Xp (i.e as a Hyperplane). When it comes to Regression, H includes models that are of the form:

$$\varphi(x) = b + \sum_{j=1}^{p} x_j w_j$$

When it comes to binary classification, we have y=({c1,c2}), H includes all models that are of the form:

$$\varphi(x) = \begin{cases} c_1 & \text{if } b + \sum_{j=1}^{p} x_j w_j > 0 \\ c_2 & \text{otherwise} \end{cases}$$

When you have a good separating hyperplane, it uses the distance to the training data points that are near.

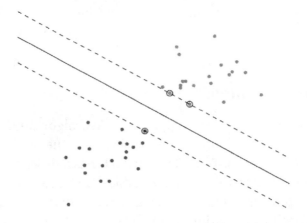

There are very many types of linear methods that differ in ways that bring about an estimation of the coefficients of b and W_j, (for j=1,...,p), it often uses specific optimization procedures that are specific to reduce the criterion. The most popular is the *least square* method. It comprises of the coefficients b and w_j which reduces the re-substitution estimate, by the use of squared error loss.

Linear methods despite their simplicity, they can provide reliable predictions and an interpretable description of how the output is affected by the input variables. Linear methods against their title can model X and Y which are nonlinear models. For instance, the application of methods used to transform variable inputs.

Support vector machines

If data points that are in a learning set are separable in a linear manner, some hyperplanes exist, which are equally good when re-substitution is evaluated. However, in generalization, the hyperplanes are usually inequivalent. As you can see in the image above, a good separation is completely achieved when the margin to the closest training data is large; when the margin is large, the model's generalization error will be low.

Support vector machine is used in max-margin linear models. If we assume that the generality loss does not exist, and we also assume that b=0 and y={-1,1}; support vector machines solve the primal optimization problem for them to be learned.

$$\min_{w, \xi} \left\{ \frac{1}{2} \|w\|^2 + C \sum_{i=1}^{N} \xi_i \right\}$$

Subject to

$$y_i \left(w \cdot x_i \right) \geq 1 - \xi_i, \quad \xi_i \geq 0.$$

The optimization problem is as below in its dual.

$$\max_{\alpha} \left\{ \sum_{i=1}^{N} \alpha_i - \frac{1}{2} \sum_{i,j} \alpha_i \alpha_j y_i y_j x_i \cdot x_j \right\}$$

This is now subject to

$$0 \leqslant \alpha_i \leqslant C,$$

C here is a hyper-parameter used to control the model's misclassification degree, in case of linearly inseparable classes. Identifying with the dual problem solution, then

$$w = \sum_{i=1}^{N} \alpha_i y_i x_i,$$

Where the expression of the linear model is done.

Support vector machines use an input space that is original, which is projected to a Kernel trick that is a high-dimension projection, in order to get to a classification that is nonlinear; the kernel trick is the place where the separating hyperplane can be found. You will be shocked to discover, that the problem found in the dual optimization is the same, but xi.xj, which is the dot product is not used. Instead, a replacement by kernel K(xi,xj) that corresponds the dot product x_i & x_j in the space that is new.

Neural Networks

The neural network family roots back to discover the mathematical representation of processing information in bio-matter. We know this is a far reaching objective; artificial neural networks have bridged the gap statistically, and it has grown to be one effective method in ML.

There are several units called neurons in a neural network. They exist in the form of

$$h_j(x) = \sigma\left(w_j + \sum_{i=1}^{n} w_{ij}x_i\right),$$

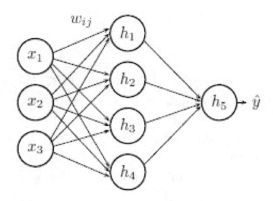

σ is an activation function that is nonlinear, just like the function of sigmoid or the activation of Softmax. In most cases, the units are laid out in successive layers, where layer inputs go towards the weighted connections which are recognized as *synapses*, to the next layer's inputs. The example on the diagram above, we are looking at a neural network that has 3 layers. The 1st layer is obviously the layer concerned with inputs which transmits the values $x=(x_1,...x_p)$ as inputs to the 2nd layer. In the 2nd layer, there are activation units h_j which take values of the input layer that are weighted, that produce outputs which are used in nonlinear transformations. Looking at the 3rd layer, it comprises of a one activation unit, that takes the weighted outputs of the 2nd layer as inputs, which then produce the predicted value $\hat{y}$. If we assume that we have a fixed structure, and all the network units utilize the identical activation function represented as σ, then the space of H hypothesis has the models represented by φ in the form:

$$\varphi(x) = \sigma\left(w_5 + \sum_{j=1}^{4} w_{j5}\sigma\left(w_j + \sum_{i=1}^{p} w_{ij}x_i\right)\right).$$

When it comes to linear methods, there is an estimation of weights w_{ij} when it comes to learning a neural network. These weights minimize the loss function but in a specific way, using optimization procedures that are specific. Among the methods, *back propagation* algorithm is the most famous method. The most advanced level of neural networks, deep learning, has proven the potential of the models to independently learn high-level data and also the representation of efficient data. On different hard tasks, like speech recognition, the neural network have accomplished greater milestones and achievements, image classification, shining past human capabilities and other automated methods.

Theoretically, it is not known as to what makes them tick. Particularly, when it comes to selecting the right combination of units, types of activation-function and layers is still a very fragile process that makes it hard for non-experts to use neural networks.

Nearest neighbor methods

These methods are of a nonparametric algorithm class. These algorithms are known as prototype methods. These methods are different because they rely on memory and they do not need to be fit in any model. They exist based on the principle of using new samples that are discovered after finding training samples that are close to them. The new sample then infers the output variable's value. When it comes to regression, the k-nearest neighbor-algorithm makes an average of the values of the output from the k closest training-samples. I.e.

$$\varphi(\mathbf{x}) = \frac{1}{k} \sum_{(\mathbf{x}_i, y_i) \in NN(\mathbf{x}, \mathcal{L}, k)} y_i,$$

In this equation, we have NN(x, L,k) as a representation of the k nearest neighbors of x in L. Classification uses the same procedure, without using the output value that is predicted which is computed as the majority class in the k nearest neighbors:

$$\varphi(x) = \arg\max_{c \in \mathcal{Y}} \sum_{(x_i, y_i) \in NN(x, \mathcal{L}, k)} 1(y_i = c).$$

The distant function that you might decide to use to identify the k-nearest neighbors has the possibility to be any kind of metric. One variant to take note of is the neighbor algorithm that is radius-based, where the output value that is predicted is calculated from the samples that are in training, which is in a new samples radius. In areas that have non-uniform sample data, the last algorithm can be a better alternative, compared to the method of the k-nearest neighbor.

Even though they are simple, nearest neighbor methods provide good results. They classify successfully, where there is an irregular decision boundary. Theoretically, the proof of the methods consistency is important. When the L size does not have an end, and k adjusts perfectly to L, the k-nearest neighbor generalization error production converges to the Bayes model generalization error.

Chapter 5: Classification of Regression Trees

We are going to look into detail the decision tree methods. We will provide an overview on how the algorithm has been developed. We will then present a mathematical presentation to introduce the notation and concepts. We will then present the learning algorithm.

Introduction

Artificial intelligence has been progressed by the curiosity of mankind who tries to understand and make use of complex data. This is through finding models that predict accurately and extract knowledge intelligently. This two sides realization has made strides in machine learning, giving rise to research in different fields. Tree based methods are by far one of the useful and effective methods that can produce understandable and reliable results on any data.

In 1963, decision trees appeared through the first tree called automatic -interaction detector which is used in the handling of non-addictive multivariate effects in the survey data. Improvements were placed on AID and more computer programs were proposed for exploratory advances.

Decision trees are now by the state of the art algorithms that includes forests or boosting methods. This is where they come in handy as building blocks for the building of large models. It is therefore important to understand the details of the algorithm of single decision trees, to analyze these methods.

Tree Structured Models

When we have finite values as the output space, like in classification, which has y={c1,c2,...,cj}, you can look at supervised leaning-problem, by noticing how Y makes a universal partition, in the universe Ω, I.e.

$\Omega = \Omega_{c1} U \Omega_{c2} ... U \Omega_{cj}$,

Ω_{ck} represents the object set where Y has C_k value. The classifier ϕ similarly, can be regarded as universe Ω partition since a definition of an approximation $\hat{y}$ of Y. The definition of the partition is however expressed using x input space, instead of Ω. I.e.

$$\mathcal{X} = \mathcal{X}^{\varphi}_{c_1} \cup \mathcal{X}^{\varphi}_{c_2} \cup ... \cup \mathcal{X}^{\varphi}_{c_j},$$

This is where $\mathcal{X}^{\varphi}_{c_k}$. is the description vectors set $x \in \mathcal{X}$ that $\phi(x) = C_k$. Learning a partition of x that matches the best partition, becomes synonymous to learning a classifier. I.e., using the model of Bayes ϕ_B over x that endangers it:

$$\mathcal{X} = \mathcal{X}_{c_1}^{\varphi_B} \cup \mathcal{X}_{c_2}^{\varphi_B} \cup \ldots \cup \mathcal{X}_{c_J}^{\varphi_B}.$$

Partitioning when there is noise

When you discover that X=x does not determine Y, where you have noise Y, then 2 objects that are distinct exist form the universe Ω. The representation x_1 and x_2 are equal in the input space, even though output values y1 and y2 are corresponding but different. H_t means that the subsets most probably will not disjoint.

$$\mathcal{X}_{c_k}^{\Omega} = \{x_i | i \in \Omega, Y = c_k\}$$

Generally, models that are tree structured are simple. It can approximate the model of Bayes partition by having the input space partitioned recursively. It uses subspaces to assign the prediction values that are constant to objects that are in the terminal subspace. For clarity, the following concepts need to be determined.

A graph G=(V, E) represents a tree that has one path that has 2 connections of node

A tree that is rooted is one that has been assigned to the root. An assumption can be made that a directed graph is the rooted tree where the nodes are directed far off the root.

When in a tree that is rooted, a node is described as internal if it has one, or more than one child.

A binary tree is a tree that is rooted and has two children in all its internal nodes.

A binary tree or a tree structure's description can be in the form of a model $\phi{:}x{\rightarrow}y$ which is then described by a binary rooted tree, where any node t is a representation of an input's space subspace, where the root node t_0 corresponds to x itself.

Induction and Decision Trees

Decision tree learning leads to determining the tree structure that produces the partition closest to the engineered partition Y over X. Decision tree construction is driven by the goal of getting a model that partitions the set of learning L in detail. From all types of decision trees, several might explain L very well. If we go by the Occam's Razor principles that prefer the explanation that makes a few assumptions, that favor a simple result that is suitable for the statistics. L is understood from a decision tree by the discovery of a small tree ϕ^*, minimizing the estimates re-substitution. From a generalization perspective, this assumption is definitive regarding interoperability. A small decision tree is easy to understand than a complex-large tree.

When you are discovering the smallest-tree ϕ^* reduces the estimation from being re-replication, this is referred to as NP-complete difficulty. As a result, when we speculate that $P{\neq}NP$, we are going to have an algorithm that is not efficient in finding ϕ^*. This suggests that the discovery of efficient heuristics that will be used in constructing near-optimal decision-trees makes it possible to have computation requirements in a realistic boundary.

For more information regarding Induction and decision trees, follow the link below

https://people.cs.umass.edu/~utgoff/papers/mlj-id5r.pdf

https://courses.cs.ut.ee/2009/bayesian-networks/extras/quinlan1986.pdf

Chapter 6: Random Forests

Bias Variance Decomposition

The error of model ϕ_L generalization is the anticipated error of prediction when you look at the loss function L

$Err(\phi_L) = E_{XY}\{L(Y, \phi_L(x))\}$

The expected error of prediction of ϕ_L at X=x can be expressed as

$$Err(\varphi_{\mathcal{L}}(\mathbf{x})) = \mathbb{E}_{Y|X=\mathbf{x}}\{L(Y, \varphi_{\mathcal{L}}(\mathbf{x}))\}.$$

When you look at regression, the loss of error squared, the result of error predicted is the anticipated disintegration of variance, a bias that comprises a useful framework for diagnosing the model's prediction error. When you get into the classifications zero-one, it is hard to obtain the same decomposition. The variance and bias concepts transpose in different ways into classification, providing frameworks that are comparable to the study of prediction classifiers error.

Regression

When you look at regression, and you assume L as the squared error loss, the model of prediction error ϕ_L at point X=x can be rephrased according to Bayes model ϕ_B:

$$\text{Err}(\varphi_{\mathcal{L}}(\mathbf{x}))$$

$$
\begin{aligned}
&= \mathbb{E}_{Y|X=x}\{(Y - \varphi_{\mathcal{L}}(\mathbf{x}))^2\} \\
&= \mathbb{E}_{Y|X=x}\{(Y - \varphi_B(\mathbf{x}) + \varphi_B(\mathbf{x}) - \varphi_{\mathcal{L}}(\mathbf{x}))^2\} \\
&= \mathbb{E}_{Y|X=x}\{(Y - \varphi_B(\mathbf{x}))^2\} + \mathbb{E}_{Y|X=x}\{(\varphi_B(\mathbf{x}) - \varphi_{\mathcal{L}}(\mathbf{x}))^2\} \\
&\hookrightarrow + \mathbb{E}_{Y|X=x}\{2(Y - \varphi_B(\mathbf{x}))(\varphi_B(\mathbf{x}) - \varphi_{\mathcal{L}}(\mathbf{x}))\} \\
&= \mathbb{E}_{Y|X=x}\{(Y - \varphi_B(\mathbf{x}))^2\} + \mathbb{E}_{Y|X=x}\{(\varphi_B(\mathbf{x}) - \varphi_{\mathcal{L}}(\mathbf{x}))^2\} \\
&= \text{Err}(\varphi_B(\mathbf{x})) + (\varphi_B(\mathbf{x}) - \varphi_{\mathcal{L}}(\mathbf{x}))^2
\end{aligned}
$$

By Bayes model regression,

$$\mathbb{E}_{Y|X=x}\{Y - \varphi_B(\mathbf{x})\} = \mathbb{E}_{Y|X=x}\{Y\} - \varphi_B(\mathbf{x}) = 0$$.

The last expression in the equation tallies with the irreducible error at X=x the 2nd term in the variation of ϕ_L taken from Bayes model. If the distance is greater from the Bayes model. The error enlarges as the sub-suitable model grows enormous.

If there is an assumption that the learning set L is a random variable and there is a deterministic learning algorithm, inconsistencies with L in the Bayes model is articulated in projecting $\mathbb{E}_L\{\phi_L(\mathbf{x})\}$ above the proficient models by understanding the feasible sets of N:

$$\mathbb{E}_{\mathcal{L}}\{(\varphi_B(x) - \varphi_{\mathcal{L}}(x))^2\}$$
$$= \mathbb{E}_{\mathcal{L}}\{(\varphi_B(x) - \mathbb{E}_{\mathcal{L}}\{\varphi_{\mathcal{L}}(x)\} + \mathbb{E}_{\mathcal{L}}\{\varphi_{\mathcal{L}}(x)\} - \varphi_{\mathcal{L}}(x))^2\}$$
$$= \mathbb{E}_{\mathcal{L}}\{(\varphi_B(x) - \mathbb{E}_{\mathcal{L}}\{\varphi_{\mathcal{L}}(x)\})^2\} + \mathbb{E}_{\mathcal{L}}\{(\mathbb{E}_{\mathcal{L}}\{\varphi_{\mathcal{L}}(x)\} - \varphi_{\mathcal{L}}(x))^2\}\}$$
$$\hookrightarrow + \mathbb{E}_{\mathcal{L}}\{2(\varphi_B(x) - \mathbb{E}_{\mathcal{L}}\{\varphi_{\mathcal{L}}(x)\})(\mathbb{E}_{\mathcal{L}}\{\varphi_{\mathcal{L}}(x)\} - \varphi_{\mathcal{L}}(x))\}$$
$$= \mathbb{E}_{\mathcal{L}}\{(\varphi_B(x) - \mathbb{E}_{\mathcal{L}}\{\varphi_{\mathcal{L}}(x)\})^2\} + \mathbb{E}_{\mathcal{L}}\{(\mathbb{E}_{\mathcal{L}}\{\varphi_{\mathcal{L}}(x)\} - \varphi_{\mathcal{L}}(x))^2\}\}$$
$$= \{\varphi_B(x) - \mathbb{E}_{\mathcal{L}}\{\varphi_{\mathcal{L}}(x)\}\}^2 + \mathbb{E}_{\mathcal{L}}\{(\mathbb{E}_{\mathcal{L}}\{\varphi_{\mathcal{L}}(x)\} - \varphi_{\mathcal{L}}(x))^2\} \qquad (4.4)$$

Since $\mathbb{E}_{\mathcal{L}}\{\mathbb{E}_{\mathcal{L}}\{\varphi_{\mathcal{L}}(x)\} - \varphi_{\mathcal{L}}(x)\} = \mathbb{E}_{\mathcal{L}}\{\varphi_{\mathcal{L}}(x)\} - \mathbb{E}_{\mathcal{L}}\{\varphi_{\mathcal{L}}(x)\} = 0.$ in conclusion, the generalization error expected decomposes additively in the theory below.

Theorem

Bias variance decomposition is from loss error squared; the anticipated generalization error $\mathbb{E}_{\mathcal{L}}\{\text{Err}\{\varphi_{\mathcal{L}}(x)\}\}$ at $X = x$ is

$$\mathbb{E}_{\mathcal{L}}\{\text{Err}\{\varphi_{\mathcal{L}}(x)\}\} = noise(x) + bias^2(x) + var(x),$$

where

$$noise(x) = \text{Err}\{\varphi_B(x)\},$$
$$bias^2(x) = \{\varphi_B(x) - \mathbb{E}_{\mathcal{L}}\{\varphi_{\mathcal{L}}(x)\}\}^2,$$
$$var(x) = \mathbb{E}_{\mathcal{L}}\{(\mathbb{E}_{\mathcal{L}}\{\varphi_{\mathcal{L}}(x)\} - \varphi_{\mathcal{L}}(x))^2\}.$$

This bias-variance-decomposition of the error of generalization was discussed in neural networks in 1992. The idiom $noise(x)$ is a lingering error. The algorithm is free of the learning set. It also provides a theoretical lower bound on the generalization error. Bias^2 makes a measure of the discrepancy between the Bayes model projection and an average projection. $var(x)$, Computes other variabilities of the X=x variations over the models.

Chapter 7: How to Interpret Random Forests

A response variable prediction based on prediction variables that are set is an important expedition in science. The aim is to make accurate response prediction; but to accurately single out predictor variables crucial in creating projections, like, for instance, is to understand the underlying process. Since they are used in many problem scenarios, and their accuracy to build models that are accurate, and in the provision of the importance measures, the major data analysis tool that I used successfully, in different scenarios is the random forests.

Despite the wide applications, there are only a few works that have looked into the algorithms theoretical and statistical mechanisms and properties.

Variable importance

When you factor in single-decision trees, the measure of importance of the variables Xj was as

$$\text{Imp}(X_j) = \sum_{t \in \varphi} \Delta I(\tilde{s}_t^j, t),$$

Where $\tilde{s}_t^j$ is the understudy split for s_t, which is a split closely defined on variable X_j that mirrors the split s_t interpreted in t node. Surrogate splits were used to account for masking-effects. However, if X_{j2} another tree is grown in place of the removal of $X_{j1,}$ then the second split may occur in the tree and split with the results may relatively be as great as the first tree. When this happens, then the relevant measure detects the X_{j2} importance.

Asymptotic analysis

A tree that is totally random and developed is a decision tree with t node being separated by the use of a variable X_j that was selected in a consistent erratic manner among the neglected parent-nodes t, that split to [Xj] sub trees.

In these trees, the depth is similar to all leaves$_p$ and those at st of grown tree is bijection with X of the feasible joint configuration of a variable. An instance is, all variable inputs are in binary, the forthcoming of the tree will have 2^p leaves.

Non-totally randomized trees

Built at random, the trees are not related to those extremely randomized trees or random forests. To comprehend the algorithms that are computed, take an alternative of node t of randomized trees, drawn equally at random $1 \leq K \leq p$ variables. Choose one that utilizes $\Delta i(t)$. Like previously, t is split to several sub-trees like the cardinality of the variable that is chosen. Know that, K=1, it aggregates to the construction of classical trees that are single in a way that is deterministic.

Chapter 8: Ensemble of Random Patches

The algorithm of random patches that is being proposed is a method that can be looked at in the following way. If you have $\mathcal{R}(\alpha_s, \alpha_f, \mathcal{L})$, that is an all random set of $\alpha_s N \times \alpha_f P$ size, which the L database is obtained from, N enumerates to the samples of L which is its input variables and $\alpha_s \in [0, 1]$ is a hyper-parameter that has control over the samples found in a patch; this shows that $\mathcal{R}(\alpha_s, \alpha_f, \mathcal{L})$ represents a set of subsets that contain $\alpha_s N$ samples that have $\alpha_f P$ variables. Below is how the method can be described.

Algorithm of Random Patches

1: **for** $m = 1, \ldots, M$ **do**
2:     Draw a patch $r \sim U(\mathcal{R}(\alpha_s, \alpha_f, \mathcal{L}))$ uniformly at random
3:     Build a model on the selected patch r
4: **end for**
5: Aggregate the predictions of the M models in an ensemble

Different base estimators can be exploited using the RP algorithm, but we are only going to consider estimators that are tree-based. RP algorithm is evaluated by the use of classification trees that are standard, as well as randomized trees that are extreme. If there is no explicit statement on the trees, the Gini index is used to grow and prune the trees as a criterion for the splitting node. The randomized trees that are extreme have parameter K, which is a set in RP of a maximum value $K = \alpha_f P$. This set does not correspond to other variables that are randomly selected.

One benefit of Random Patches is that it makes a generalization of Pasting Rvotes together with the algorithm of Random Subspace. Both of these cases are cases of the setting of RP $\alpha_s = 1.0$ which yields RS, as set $\alpha_f = 1.0$ produces P. When hyper-parameters α_s and α_f are simultaneously turned, RP is expected to be as good as the methods seen. The only requirement is that in the tuning instance, over-fitting is not allowed.

Level decision trees that have base estimators, there are parallels that can be derived from RF and RP algorithms. For $\alpha_s = 1.0,$ value of $\alpha_f P$ is almost equal to K feature numbers that are assessed node splitting occurs. There is a difference that still exists. Subsets features in RP are globally selected at once, before a tree construction. On the contrary, RF subset features are derived from each local node. It is clear that the RP approach can be used easily when one is working with huge databases. One does not need to consider features that are not selected. This now lowers the memory needs that are needed when a tree is being built. One other interesting parallel happens when there is the use of bootstrap samples, like how it is used in RF. A set $\alpha_s = 0.632,$ is normally close. This is an indication of the proportion averaging of samples that are unique in a sample bootstrap. The differences that exist are such that, in bootstrap samples, the unique samples that are being trained vary, compared to RP that has fixed 0.632N. The other difference is in the unequal weights of the samples in bootstrap.

Additionally, RP is related to the algorithms referred to as SubBag, which is known to combine RS and Bagging for the ensembles construction. When samples of N boot-strapped that were almost equal to $\alpha_s = 0.632,$ and $\alpha_f = 0.75,$ it was proposed that the performance of SubBag is much more, compared to RF's performance. One RF's advantage is that it applies to any base estimator.

Accuracy Needs

The validation we have seen of RP algorithm is done in 2steps. We need to first look at how RP stacks to other ensemble methods that are tree based, in the context of accuracy. We then need to look at its memory requirements in order to achieve accuracy and also to determine the capability of the algorithm to take charge of memory constraints that are strong; this is also compared to alternative ensemble methods.

When you are looking at accuracy α_s and α_f give off degrees of freedom that are considered. It is to remarkably improve or reduce RP's performance. On a first impression basis, it is possible for one to presume that due to base estimators being built on parts of data, the ensembles accuracy will be low if you compare it with the whole set used to construct the base estimators. Our aim is to see if the features that are being sampled globally, lower their performance, compared to local sampling. This is now the main difference between the more modern RF, and the more old school RP.

Protocol

Comparison of our method is done with RS, RF, and P. 2 variant considerations have been considered for P, RS, and RP. One variant uses decision trees that are standard, as base estimators, while the other uses base estimators of randomized trees that are extreme. In general, the comparison takes place in 8 methods. RP-DT, P-ET, P-DT, RS-ET, RF, ET, RS-DT, and RP-ET.

The method's accuracy is calculated using a list that is extensive, which has both classification and artificial problems. 3 random partitions exist in every data set: the 1st and bigger half of the actual data set is for training: 2nd 25% is for validation and the last 25% is for testing. Hyper-parameters α_s and α_f in all methods were tuned with grid-search procedures on the set of validation. The grid that was used was {0.01, 0.1..., 0.9, 1.0} for α_s and α_f. Default values were given to the other hyper-parameters. In ET and RF, the selected features of K are chosen at random at each node, tuned by the use of $\alpha_r p$ grid. If one was to look at all the ensembles, two hundred and fifty trees that flourished were produced; with a generalization of the estimated set of testing. The procedure repetition was done 50 times, for all methods and data sets. This was done by the use of the fifty random partitions that were used in the methods.

Data sets that are small

We need to try out our approach on the data sets that are small, before going into heavy experimentation. To achieve this, experiments have been carried out on sixteen public data sets that will be seen in *Table 1* below, which was found in a repository of a machine learning in UCI. The data sets obtained cover a number of conditions, as well as the range of sample sizes, that start from 208 and end up at 20000, and the variable features range from 6 up to 168. *Table 2* below has a detailed performance of the eight methods for all sixteen data sets, with the help of the protocol that has been discussed above. We are going to make an analysis of the trends by conducting several tests of statistics.

First, we performed the Friedman test rebating the theory detailing the equality of each and every algorithm at a crucial level $\alpha = 0.05.$ Then we did the Nemenyi test, to compare the pairwise of the eight-methods average ranking. This test showed that 2 classifiers are different $(at\ \alpha = 0.05),$ if there is a difference in their ranking average, by at minimum the critical difference = 2.6249.

Table 1

Dataset	N	p
DIABETES	768	8
DIG44	18000	16
IONOSPHERE	351	34
PENDIGITS	10992	16
LETTER	20000	16
LIVER	345	6
MUSK2	6598	168
RING-NORM	10000	20
SATELLITE	6435	36
SEGMENT	2310	19
SONAR	208	60
SPAMBASE	4601	57
TWO-NORM	9999	20
VEHICLE	1692	18
VOWEL	990	10
WAVEFORM	5000	21

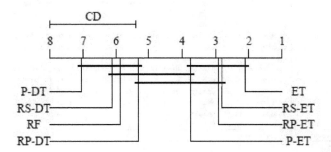

Figure1: Average ranking of small data sets and methods

Figure 1 makes a summary of the comparisons. The line at the top is the axis where the average tank R_m is plotted in each model, from the worst methods (highest rank) that are on the left side, to the best method (lowest rank) that is on the right. Statistically, similar method groups are connected together. Critical Difference is well exhibited in the diagram above. To support the ranking comparisons we have looked at, a 50 accuracy comparison is done over each split of data set for each method, by the use of a paired t-test (with $\alpha = 0.01$). The comparison results are then summarized in the table below in the context of 'Win-Draw-Loss' method pair statuses. When you see the intersection of 3 values of column j and row i, it shows the number of data set methods i is not different than j method.

Validation	RF	ET	P-DT	P-ET	RS-DT	RS-ET	RP-DT	RP-ET
DIABETES	77.12 (6)	77.25 (5)	77.67 (4)	78.01 (3)	75.11 (8)	76.77 (7)	78.82 (2)	79.07 (1)
DIG44	94.99 (7)	95.78 (1)	91.86 (8)	95.46 (4)	95.07 (6)	95.69 (3)	95.13 (5)	95.72 (2)
IONOSPHERE	94.40 (6)	95.15 (3)	93.86 (8)	94.75 (5)	94.11 (7)	94.90 (4)	95.20 (2)	95.36 (1)
PENDIGITS	98.94 (7)	99.33 (1)	98.09 (8)	99.28 (4)	99.02 (6)	99.31 (3)	99.07 (5)	99.32 (2)
LETTER	95.36 (7)	96.38 (1)	92.72 (8)	95.87 (4)	95.68 (6)	96.08 (3)	95.74 (5)	96.10 (2)
LIVER	72.37 (5)	71.90 (6)	72.55 (4)	72.88 (3)	68.06 (8)	70.88 (7)	74.53 (1)	74.37 (2)
MUSK2	97.18 (7)	97.73 (1)	96.89 (8)	97.60 (4)	97.58 (6)	97.72 (3)	97.60 (5)	97.73 (2)
RING-NORM	97.44 (6)	98.10 (5)	96.41 (8)	97.28 (7)	98.25 (4)	98.41 (3)	98.50 (2)	98.54 (1)
SATELLITE	90.97 (7)	91.56 (1)	90.01 (8)	91.40 (5)	91.31 (6)	91.50 (3)	91.41 (4)	91.54 (2)
SEGMENT	97.46 (6)	98.17 (2)	96.78 (8)	98.10 (4)	97.33 (7)	98.14 (3)	97.52 (5)	98.21 (1)
SONAR	82.92 (7)	86.92 (3)	80.03 (8)	84.73 (5)	83.07 (6)	87.07 (2)	85.42 (4)	88.15 (1)
SPAMBASE	94.80 (7)	95.36 (3)	93.69 (8)	95.01 (6)	95.01 (5)	95.50 (2)	95.11 (4)	95.57 (1)
TWO-NORM	97.54 (6)	97.77 (2)	97.52 (7)	97.59 (5)	97.46 (8)	97.63 (4)	97.76 (3)	97.82 (1)
VEHICLE	88.67 (5)	88.68 (4)	88.26 (8)	88.74 (3)	88.41 (7)	88.60 (6)	89.22 (1)	89.21 (2)
VOWEL	92.04 (5)	95.12 (1)	85.19 (8)	93.49 (4)	89.76 (7)	94.34 (3)	91.10 (6)	94.48 (2)
WAVEFORM	85.45 (6)	85.96 (2)	84.89 (8)	85.68 (5)	84.91 (7)	85.69 (4)	85.85 (3)	86.21 (1)
Average rank	6.25	2.5625	7.4375	4.4375	6.5	3.75	3.5626	1.5

Test	RF	ET	P-DT	P-ET	RS-DT	RS-ET	RP-DT	RP-ET
DIABETES	75.62 (4)	75.38 (5)	75.67 (3)	76.34 (1)	73.03 (8)	74.63 (7)	75.32 (6)	75.82 (2)
DIG44	94.96 (6)	95.67 (1)	91.79 (8)	95.39 (4)	94.98 (5)	95.58 (2)	94.95 (7)	95.55 (3)
IONOSPHERE	92.20 (6)	93.22 (1)	92.09 (7)	92.40 (4)	92.02 (8)	93.22 (2)	92.34 (5)	92.68 (3)
PENDIGITS	98.84 (7)	99.23 (1)	97.97 (8)	99.21 (3)	98.95 (5)	99.21 (2)	98.93 (6)	99.20 (4)
LETTER	95.27 (7)	96.29 (1)	92.57 (8)	95.89 (4)	95.61 (5)	96.03 (2)	95.61 (6)	95.99 (3)
LIVER	69.95 (3)	68.22 (6)	70.43 (1)	69.58 (5)	63.17 (8)	67.35 (7)	70.20 (2)	69.67 (4)
MUSK2	97.08 (7)	97.61 (1)	96.69 (8)	97.54 (4)	97.47 (5)	97.58 (2)	97.42 (6)	97.56 (3)
RING-NORM	97.48 (6)	98.07 (5)	96.42 (8)	97.25 (7)	98.16 (4)	98.31 (1)	98.22 (3)	98.30 (2)
SATELLITE	90.67 (7)	91.22 (2)	89.66 (8)	91.20 (3)	91.15 (5)	91.28 (1)	91.04 (6)	91.20 (4)
SEGMENT	97.02 (5)	97.93 (1)	96.44 (8)	97.86 (3)	96.86 (7)	97.90 (2)	96.88 (6)	97.84 (4)
SONAR	79.53 (5)	82.76 (1)	75.15 (8)	80.07 (4)	78.50 (6)	82.19 (2)	78.26 (7)	81.92 (3)
SPAMBASE	94.76 (7)	95.17 (3)	93.51 (8)	94.84 (5)	94.88 (4)	95.22 (2)	94.80 (6)	95.22 (1)
TWO-NORM	97.22 (7)	97.50 (1)	97.26 (6)	97.29 (4)	97.20 (8)	97.33 (2)	97.33 (3)	97.28 (5)
VEHICLE	87.47 (7)	87.85 (3)	87.01 (8)	87.98 (2)	87.50 (6)	87.68 (5)	87.73 (4)	88.08 (1)
VOWEL	91.51 (5)	93.95 (1)	84.17 (8)	92.93 (4)	89.51 (7)	93.60 (2)	89.89 (6)	93.09 (3)
WAVEFORM	85.23 (5)	85.77 (1)	84.68 (8)	85.40 (3)	84.74 (7)	85.38 (4)	85.16 (6)	85.56 (2)
Average rank	5.875	2.125	7.0625	3.75	6.125	2.8125	5.3125	2.9375

Table 2: Percentage accuracy on small data sets

	RF	ET	P-DT	P-ET	RS-DT	RS-ET	RP-DT	RP-ET
RF	—	1/2/13	12/4/0	1/7/8	4/7/5	2/2/12	1/10/5	0/4/12
ET	13/2/1	—	14/1/1	10/5/1	13/3/0	4/11/1	12/2/2	5/10/1
P-DT	0/4/12	1/1/14	—	0/4/12	2/3/11	2/1/13	0/4/12	0/4/12
P-ET	8/7/1	1/5/10	12/4/0	—	9/6/1	2/6/8	9/6/1	0/11/5
RS-DT	5/7/4	0/3/13	11/3/2	1/6/9	—	0/2/14	1/11/4	0/4/12
RS-ET	12/2/2	1/11/4	13/1/2	8/6/2	14/2/0	—	11/4/1	1/13/2
RP-DT	5/10/1	2/2/12	12/4/0	1/6/9	4/11/1	1/4/11	—	0/6/10
RP-ET	12/4/0	1/10/5	12/4/0	5/11/0	12/4/0	2/13/1	10/6/0	—

Table 3: Pairwise t-tests comparison on small data sets

Average accuracies are not different between methods. Even though this is the case, there is some noticeable trend that appears when one is looking at *Table 1* and *Table 3*. First, ET techniques are first positioned, then DT methods that include RF algorithm. Generally, the RT algorithm comes first in ranking $R_{ET}=2.125$, and RP-ET and RS-ET follow closely at positions $R_{RP-ET}=2.9375$ and $R_{RS-ET}=2.8125$ while trailing behind, we have P-ET, $R_{P-ET}=3.75$.

When you look at *Table 1*, it is ET that is ranked higher than the other DT methods. But when you look at the ET variant that is worse, P-ET maintains at nine times on a better level and one time worse than RP-DT, which is the best variant of DT. The disparity between these algorithms now becomes evident. It is now clear that when you use split thresholds that are random, instead of decision trees that are examples of optimized ones, then it pays off in the generalization context.

When you look at ET methods, RP-ET is favored to P-ET, though it is not as good as RS-ET and ET in average ranking. Because RS-ET is an RP-ET case, it is recommended that there is over-fitting when the additional parameter α_s is being tuned. RP-ET is indeed ranked better, compared to RS-ET on the validation set. *Table 3* shows otherwise and, it shows that RP-ET is better compared to RS-ET (2/13/1). When you look at ET instead of RP-ET, the performance of ET (5/10/1) is solely because subsets of ET features are re-derived locally on every node during tree construction, and not a one size fits all before the tree construction. This leads to a lower chance of generation of trees that are improper, because of initial features that are bad, leading to a better accuracy and a lower bias.

When you look at DT methods, RP-DT is first, with a mean of 5.3125, followed by RF (R_{RF}=5.875), then RS-DT R_{RS-DT}=6.125 finally AT P-DT, which is R_{P-DT}=7.0625.

Data sets that are larger

The experiments we have seen above yield some potential results, it is then fair to see if it is possible to see conclusions and generalizations on larger problems, for instance, when you are exposed to features that are hidden in thousands or genomic or non-important data. You can also try to see if it is possible to deal with features that are correlated, like images. To look into this, a 2nd experiment was conducted on thirteen large data sets, in *Table 4*. *Madelon* is the only data that is not real. When you look at the dimensions, the data sets are big and they get to thousands of samples and quite a number of features. This means that the complexity of the problem is expected to be bigger. The same protocol that was used in smaller data sets was used here. Now, to make sure that the computing times were lower on data sets that had a mark *, the methods were parsed using a hundred trees instead of two hundred and fifty, with the minimum no. of samples needed in each internal model set to 10, to manage complexity. The results are as seen in *Table 5,* and a summary of *Table 2* and *Table 6*. This is in relation to the average rank, with a critical difference at $\alpha = 0.05$, and Win/DRAW/Loss that have paired test.

After looking at *Figure 1,* it is clear that the average ranks are closer to the other in the experiment seen above. In this experiment, they are ranging from 2.38 to 6.61, while in the previous experiment, it ranges from 2.12 - 7. There is more connection with methods using critical-difference-bars. This shows how similar they are than before.

Chapter 9: Introduction of Decision Trees

Learning decision trees is an inductive reference that uses experiential techniques. The approximated detached value function that makes the data reliable and it is possible for one to learn expressions that are disjunctive.

The learning of Decision trees can approximate target functions that are discrete-valued. Learning trees can be re-represented and the readability upgraded. This is a famous inductive inference algorithm that has been applied successfully to various tasks from learning the diagnosis of medical issues to learning the access loan application risk when done on credit.

Representation of Decision tree

They are classified by decision trees that group them from starting of the tree which is the root to the leaf node. This provides a categorization of the instances. Tree nodes are a specialty in instances' experiment, with branches falling from the node to be in tune with a workable attribute value.

An example is a classification beginning at the nodes of the root of the tree; giving the specified attribute at the node a chance, descending the branch of the tree that tallies with the value of the attribute. The node has a rooted sub-tree where the procedure is repeated, that is new.

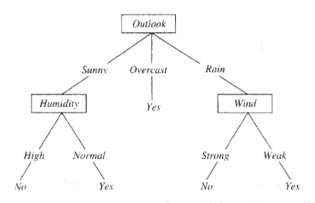

The decision tree placed above it a tennis playing concept.

In the figure above, we can see is a decision tree that is learned, and it is used to classify Saturday mornings depending on the wealth that is convenient for tennis ball playing. For instance

(Wind=Strong, Temperature=Hot, Outlook=Sunny, Humidity=High)

This can be sorted out down in the left part of the decision tree's branch that is above, the chance of it to be considered an instance would be regarded as an instance that is negative. That is, there is a tree prediction that says playing tennis is a no. Generally, there is a representation of decision trees of conjunctions and disjunction of limitations on the occurrences' trait esteems. Every way begins from the tree base of a leaf to relating to characteristic tests conjunction, and the tree setting off to a disjunction of the conjunctions. For example, the tree in the diagram above goes along with the expression

$$(Outlook = Sunny \land Humidity = Normal)$$
$$\lor \quad (Outlook = Overcast)$$
$$\lor \quad (Outlook = Rain \land Wind = Weak)$$

Problems that are appropriate for decision-tree learning

There are multiple selection-tree studying strategies which might be created with differing necessities and skills. Decision-tree getting to know is usually applicable flawlessly to issues with the characteristics:

The target function contains output values that are discrete

The decision-tree we have seen assigns boolean classifications, for instance, a no or a yes for the particular instance. Decision-tree techniques reach to functions of learning functions having more than 2 output values. Learning target functions are allowed by a more stable extension that has actual-valued outputs, even though the decision-tree utility is not common.

Instances are represented by attribute-value pairs.

A fixed group of attributes describes an instance; we have 'hot' values for 'Temperature'. Decision tree learning can be accredited to every attribute considered by some disjointed values, for instance, mild, cold and hot. However, the extension allows for the algorithm to be managed with actual valued attributes, like Temperature.

Disjunctive descriptions can be a necessity. Decision trees commonly are a representation of expressions that are disjunctive.

Errors may be present in the training data. Decision-tree studying techniques might have huge errors, training instances that are in the classification errors and also in attributed values which instances are defined.

Study data with attribute values missing. Decision tree practice used when some illustrations of training having figures that are unknown. For instance, if the day's humidity is known for some training examples only.

Lots of practical problems have been discovered to fit this characteristic. Problems have been exposed to decision-tree learning like the classification of patients by the disease they are suffering from, the cause of malfunctions of the equipment, the likelihood of loan applicants depending on their repayment rate. These problems, where the task is the classification that looks at a particular set of categories, is what is known as *categorization problems.*

Decision tree studying basic algorithm

Many algorithms available are for decision-tree learning for a variation of the algorithm which is considered to the core, which employs a search that is top-down through possible decision-tree space. The approach we have seen is present in the ID3 algorithm which has a successor. This now forms a discussion.

The ID3 algorithms, using a top-down construction approach, learn the decision trees by starting with the question "what should be tested as the root of the tree? What is to be tested as the tree's root?" Every attribute instance is analyzed by an experiment that is statistical, used to determine how classification is well done in the studying examples. The applied attribute is chosen to be utilized to test the node in the root of the tree. The establishment of the node at the root's successor is done and made accessible to every attribute's value possibility, and studying samples distributed to the respective node descendant. The whole procedure is then started all over again with examples that are associated with the descendant in each node, to select the attribute that can be tested at each tree's point.

Space search Hypothesis in learning decision trees

Just like the other inductive methods of learning, ID3 can be looked at having a characteristic of space searching of a hypothesis that trains instances. The ID3 space searched hypothesis is done by some potential decision trees. ID3 does an increasing difficulty, hill-climbing hunt through the present theorem, to begin with, is an empty tree, and going ahead to consider growing hypothesis that is elaborated in the discovery of a decision that can classify training data correctly. The function of evaluation that helps in the hill-climbing is the gain measure of the information. This has been depicted in the figure below.

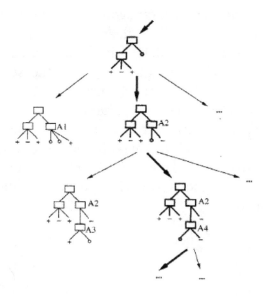

This diagram contains ID3 space search. ID3 looks for potential decision-trees in the space, from the simple to the more advanced guide by the use of the information heuristic.

When you view ID3 regarding its search strategy & search space, insight can be derived from its capabilities and disadvantages.

The hypothesis that is found in ID3 of decision trees is a dedicated area of endless discrete-valued purpose, corresponding to attributes that are available. As every limited discrete-valued task is likely to be represented by a couple of decision tree, ID3 evades some big risk of methods that search hypothesis that is incomplete.

ID3 has one present thesis going through the area of decision trees. It is collateral, an instance is the means of eliminating candidates, it is an earlier space version, it sticks with the story that the set of the constituent hypothesis has the training examples that are available. In the determination of 1 hypothesis, ID3 sheds off the capacities that allow in the explicit representation of all the hypothesis. For example, no ability to stand to determine the decision trees that are alternative and steady with the studying data that is provided.

Inductive bias in the learning of decision trees

What policy does ID3 generalize from training examples that have been observed to classify instances that are unseen? What question it began is that what is the inductive bias? When you have training examples that are collected, there are decision trees that mesh well with the examples. Describing the inductive ID3 bias points to the rationale in which selection is done in relation to theories placed. They have to reoccur more frequently than others. Which ID3 is selected by the decision-trees? The 1st tree that is acceptable is selected, and it communicates within its increasing in difficulty-hill-climbing exploration, to go through the ideal trees' space. Logically, the combing through a strategy of the ID3.

Insights on Random Forests

We are going to look at the importance of variables which are calculated from random forests. We will look at the importance of redundant variables, then we look at importance of variables when you are working with ordered variables and decision trees that are binary. Using this structure, we will look at the different sources of the bias that may happen concurrently in the computation of importance from random forests. Let us dive into the mathematics behind importance and random forests.

Inessential Variables

In most cases, the input variables in machine learning issues are parallel to each other. They also share a little bit of mutual information. This can be explained with image classification; the pixels are individual, yet they are highly parallel and individually do give or have similar information as those of their neighbors. With this in mind, variables can be partially parallel, that is, they might share some information with each other on the variable output Y.

In the extreme, unnecessariness is either complete or total. As some variables may show some excess and similar data variable output Y. To help us understand this, let's look at an example of variable inputs and the effect adding redundant variables has on randomized trees.

Two variables X_i and X_j are not required if only one can explain the other and likewise. To define redundancy:

If no additional data is needed to describe the two variables, then they are considered redundant. This means, if:

$$H(X_i|X_j) = H(X_j|X_i) = 0.$$

This is expressed if X_j and its duplicate X'_j are extremely inessential. Concerning random forests, replicates of variables if added, the split selection would not be affected. Irrespective of some redundant variables split is chosen the same, always. It does not matter if the division will be replicated severally.

Basing any of the structure generated decision trees is as a result of having a simultaneous decline in the probability of the variables being selected. Duplicated variable's nature has a huge impact on accuracy's effect. X_j has more data about the input, the splits being favored on this variable through copies being added, can lead to increase in efficiency. Over-fitting may be a result of additional copies being introduced if X_j is unrelated.

On the subject of variable importance, effects of redundant variables being added can be obtained

Quantitatively as well as qualitatively. Copies of relevant variables being added affect the importance of the replicated variable; additionally the significance of the variables is left.

Let us presume that $V = \{X_1, ..., X_p\}$ set of input variables and output Y, are computed from developed and randomized trees that are built on an enormous limitless data set. It'll be for conditioning set B:

$$I(X_i; Y|B, X_j) = I(X_j; Y|B, X_i) = 0$$
$$I(X_i; Y|B) = I(X_j; Y|B).$$

The data symmetry will be

$$I(X_i; X_j) = H(X_i) - H(X_i|X_j)$$
$$= H(X_j) - H(X_j|X_i),$$

With $H(X_i) = H(X_j)$ as $H(X_i|X_j) = H(X_i|X_j) = 0$ if the variables are redundant. As $0 \leqq H(X_i|X_j, B) \leqq H(X_i|X_j)$ and $H(X_i|X_j) = 0$. There also $H(X_i|X_j, B) = 0$.

When the argument is repeated for $I(X_i;X_j|B)$ in preference to $I(X_i;X_j)$.

Equality, in this case, carries onto any B set conditioned. As $H(X_i|B) = H(X_j|B)$ and from here, it will go on to:

$$I(X_i;Y|B,X_j) = H(X_i|B,X_j) - H(X_i|B,X_j,Y) = 0 - 0,$$
$$I(X_j;Y|B,X_i) = H(X_j|B,X_i) - H(X_j|B,X_i,Y) = 0 - 0,$$

And it can proceed to

$$\begin{aligned}
I(X_i;Y|B) &= H(X_i|B) - H(X_i|B,Y) \\
&= H(X_j|B) - H(X_j|B,Y) \\
&= I(X_j;Y|B),
\end{aligned}$$

Several propositions can be used here for instance: Proposition 1: If $X_j \in V$ is a relevant variable in connection with Y and V. If $X'_j \notin V$ is an incredibly redundant variable respecting X_j. Sample size of X_j computed with endless ensemble of totally randomized and developed random trees built $V \cup X'_j\}$ is

$$\begin{aligned}
Imp(X_j) &= \sum_{k=0}^{p-1+1} \frac{1}{C_{p+1}^k} \frac{1}{p+1-k} \sum_{B \in \mathcal{P}_k(V^{-j} \cup \{X'_j\})} I(X_j;Y|B) \\
&= \sum_{k=0}^{p-1} \frac{1}{C_{p+1}^k} \frac{1}{p+1-k} \sum_{B \in \mathcal{P}_k(V^{-j})} I(X_j;Y|B) \\
&= \sum_{k=0}^{p-1} \frac{p-k}{p+1} \frac{1}{C_p^k} \frac{1}{p-k} \sum_{B \in \mathcal{P}_k(V^{-j})} I(X_j;Y|B),
\end{aligned}$$

The importance of X_j decreased when X'_j, a redundant variable is added to input variables as a factor $\frac{p-k}{p+1} < 1$ replicates all information terms. Inherently, the result is anticipated since data is similar and is relayed within the confines of the two variables, that is, X_j and X'_j, its duplicate. The terms of importance are not entirely amended similarly. The weight of small conditioning sets is unchanged as those of terms with p being the large number and k representing small numbers; p-k/p+1 tends to be close to 1. While large conditioning sets have the likelihood of their weight being affected; that is large values of p-k/p+1 is 0.

Another proposition would be: Endless sample size $X_l \in V^{-j}$ is evaluated with infinite ensemble of randomized trees that are built on $V \cup \{X'_j\}$ as

$$Imp(X_1) = \sum_{k=0}^{p-2} \frac{p-k}{p+1} \frac{1}{C_p^k} \frac{1}{p-k} \sum_{B \in \mathcal{P}_k(V^{-l} \setminus X_j)} I(X_1; Y|B) + \quad (7.16)$$

$$\hookrightarrow \sum_{k=0}^{p-2} \left[\sum_{k'=1}^{2} \frac{C_2^{k'}}{C_{p+1}^{k+k'}} \frac{1}{p+1-(k+k')} \right] \sum_{B \in \mathcal{P}_k(V^{-l} \setminus X_j)} I(X_1; Y|B \cup X_j).$$

Effects of adding X_j, which is a redundant variable, and its importance on other variables X_l as $l \neq j$, is twofold.

In general, it is best if caution is applied when dealing with the interpretation of variable importance scores. As a result of redundancy effects because of total or partial, that often occurs during practice; the overall importance of the provided variable can be misguidedly small or highly misleading. This is because the same data is distributed within a couple of redundant variables which can be accounted for, within the total importance, several times.

It is, therefore, advisable to complement the interpretation with the variable scores being systematically decomposed. This will help immensely in understanding the reason why variables are important and how to detect redundancy conceivably.

Prejudice in Variable Importance

Variable importance is influenced immensely due to the masking effects, tree structure, and the impurity misestimations. These factors, later on, make the variable importance to deviate from possible results that are found in conditions referred to as asymptotic, that are in trees that are entirely randomized.

i. Partiality as a result of masking effects.

It has been known that decision trees that are constructed with randomization being too much tend to increase biases, respecting generalization error that compensation is involved as a result of variance decrease. Thus, K (which is a split variable for K>1) has to be adjusted accordingly to get the suitable trade-off.

Though there are instances, for example, if a variable selection is not random meaning, K>1, the masking effects that result in a bias about variable importance. Some branches are forced to entirely not built; therefore, some conditioning sets B $\in \mathcal{P}(V)$ are not considered. The result of such actions leads to random forests with the K as their parameter being tuned to make full use of accuracy that could yield variable importance that are one-sided or under- or overestimated.

Another instance can be having relevant variables that are null concerning its importance. Thus, it is indistinguishable from other irrelevant variables thus making the relevant variables dependent on some extraneous variables. This can be explained in the table below:

X_1		$\sim N(0, 1)$
X_2		$\sim M(2)$
X_3		$\sim M(4)$
X_4		$\sim M(10)$
X_5		$\sim M(20)$
null case	Y	$\sim B(0.5)$
power case	$Y\vert X_2 = 0$	$\sim B(0.5 - \text{relevance})$
	$Y\vert X_2 = 1$	$\sim B(0.5 + \text{relevance})$

The table shows the input variables that are independent random variables with:

- $N(0,1)$ the standard normal distribution

- *M(k) as the multinomial distribution with values ranging in {0,...,k- 1}* and probabilities being equal

- $B(p)$ the binomial distribution

- When considering the null case, Y is dependent from $X_1,..., X_5$. Power case Y depends on X_2 value with the rest of the input variables being irrelevant.

ii. Bias because of Empirical Impurity Estimations

Analysis of variable importance has shown how asymptotic conditions, what identifies the impurity of an actual node are alleged to be acknowledged. But in practice, impurity measurements are afflicted with empirical misestimation bias. Node impurity misestimation is directly proportional to split variable cardinality, and the Number N_t samples that are used is inversely proportional to it. This results in a reduction in impurities that have been overestimated as the tree and the variables are largely due to some values. There are ramifications that occur afterward. The variable importance is affected by bias as the variables end up being cardinally higher and of more importance, which is a mistake.

Evaluating impurity on samples that are small eventually lead to mutual information being overestimated and variable importance being biased. More specifically, the high cardinality of variable leads to misestimations being large.

The ways to reduce the chances of this recurring is by halting early construction of tree or by making the leaves grow at a slower rate than size N, used on the learning set. To reduce over-estimations, do not use variable selection when evaluating variables' relevance.

In conclusion, trees that are built at maximum depth, larger than the relevant variables' number r, and stopping early construction of trees does not necessarily hinder us from identifying relevant variables.

iii. Threshold selection and Binary trees biases

In practice, we realize that random forests depend heavily on binary splits instead of multi-way splits. When it comes to impurity, it concludes to distinct and bonus data terms that earlier were not regarded due to;

i.   Binary splits detach the data that is a variable

ii.   A similar variable is capable of being reused severally and its branch as well

These make the variable importance rely on split threshold assortment strategy. If a demanding theoretical framework lacks, the segment receives preliminary insights on the variable importance that can be found on binary decision trees. This might help in understanding their interpretation.

To understand this better, here's an example.

Toy classification problem that is made of ternary input variable X_1 and X_2 as the binary input variable with the two being ordered. It can be presumed that the data samples have been drawn equally defining the output as $Y = X_1 < X_2$ as a duplicate of Y. Concerning Y, the variables are informative, and they are expected for it to be a similar case with their importance. Exhaustive splits and randomized trees, there is the possibility of two equally probable decision trees to be built.

From:

$$\text{Imp}(X_1) = \frac{1}{2}I(X_1;Y) = \frac{1}{2}H(Y) = 0.459,$$

$$\text{Imp}(X_2) = \frac{1}{2}I(X_2;Y) = \frac{1}{2}H(Y) = 0.459.$$

You then get to make the samples that are equiprobable like shown below:

y	x_1	x_2
0	0	0
1	1	1
1	2	1

The randomized trees that are going to be built based on the samples above to get decision trees that are also equiprobable are going to be projected in this manner:

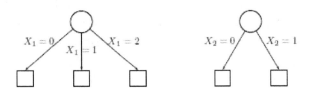

When binary splits and ETs that is K = 1, are used, resulting in varying decision trees:

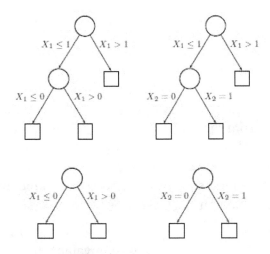

From the results above, the decision trees are being generated with a probability of (from left to right, top to bottom) 1/8, 1/8, 1/4 and 1/2. These results show that X_2 is of much importance than X_1.

To help with understanding the outcome above, the X_1 root node is split; showing that the binary roots have equal probability:

$$t_L = X_1 \leqslant 0, t_R = X_1 > 0 \text{ or } t_L = X_1 \leqslant 1, t_R = X_1 > 1.$$

Previously, the child nodes that occurred were pure thus bringing to a standstill the construction process. In the most recent case, the corresponding $X_1 > 1$, which is the right child, is pure while the child on the left is not. In this particular node, the recurring partitioning goes on, so that the second binary split is simple on X_1 and X_2. The asymptotic conditions are in the binary trees as measured variable importance:

$$\text{Imp}(X_1) = \frac{2}{8}I(X_1 \leqslant 1; Y) + \frac{1}{8}P(X_1 \leqslant 1)I(X_1 \leqslant 0; Y|X_1 \leqslant 1) + \frac{1}{4}I(X_1 \leqslant 0; Y)$$
$$= 0.375$$
$$\text{Imp}(X_2) = \frac{1}{2}I(X_2; Y) + \frac{1}{8}P(X_1 \leqslant 1)I(X_2; Y|X_1 \leqslant 1)$$
$$= 0.541,$$

This differentiates them from importance that are gathered from the multi-way totally randomized trees. The importance is accountable for the conditioning sets as a result of binarization of split variables; which might also have some values that are found in the same variable. An example would be X_2 importance includes $I(X_2; Y|X_1 \leqslant 1)$, which translates to shared data between X_2 and Y; if X_1 is equivalent to 0 or 1. Conditioning sets are not considered in multi-way exhaustive splits due to the branches concurring to values that are singular only. Standard information terms like $I(X_1 \leq 1; Y)$ are taken into account by importance as well. It is best to understand that the randomized trees aren't accounted for due to the multi-way splits.

Variable importance are affected by binary splits through the threshold selection as the control of how binarization of primary variables occurs. Intermediate variables v are plausible in ETs, which result in combinatorial number on the additional impurity terms $I(X_j < v^*; Y|\cdot)$ and $I(\cdot; Y|X_j < v^*, \cdot)$ as this masks the rest.

A final example to show this is the variable importance for X_1 and X_2 that occur when cardinality increases $L = |X_1|$ for X_1 that can be seen on the toy problem. To redefine output as $Y = X_1 < L/2$, for $X_1 = \{0, ..., L - 1\}$, as X_2 is retained as binary variable that is classified as a duplicate of Y. Hypothetically speaking, in case the input samples are equiprobable, importance that are yielded by the randomized trees remain as before if they have multiway split. ETs are different though, L increases bring about more impurity terms that are new and are being taken into account when considering importance. Below, the figure does indicate the growth in cardinality of X_1 that results in the decrease of importance while simultaneously increasing X_2 importance. X_2 splitting always leads to child nodes that are pure which is not the case for X_1, when it is split randomly.

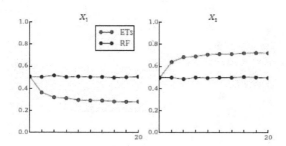

This shows the increase in cardinality of X_1 on the variable importance of X_1 and X_2.

Additional effects that are a result of binary splits generate variable importance from classical random forests. These are quite difficult to comprehend and elucidate as the information that contains several variables from a variety of categories. It is possible to identify the relevant variables with the data acquired, be cautious when clarifying importance amplitude. With the last example, there can be either misleadingly high or low due to the combinatorial effects. This is because of the possible ways variables can be binarized through the implementation of threshold selection mechanisms.

Summary

We would like to recommend you to look at the book Learning for Absolute Beginners: *A simple, Concise, and Complete Introduction to Supervised and Unsupervised Learning Algorithms.* This is with the aim of learning the basics of the following concepts as discussed in this book:

- Algorithmic types of Supervised learning

    - Bayesian Networks

    -Neural Networks

    -K-means algorithm

    -Perceptron

    -Logical regression

    - Boosting

- Step by step process of supervised learning

- Learning more about Back propagation algorithm

- Self-Organization Map (SOM)

- Advantages of SOM

- The difference between Supervised and Unsupervised Learning

Conclusion

Thank you for making it through to the end of *Machine Learning for Beginners: The Definitive Guide to Neural Networks, Random Forests, and Decision Trees*, let us hope that the information provided in this book was able to provide you with the skills in understanding how Neural Networks perform. We hope that you are now inspired in getting into learning the code and creating neural networks after understanding how they function. Reading this book is not the end of the road, it's just the beginning.

The next step you should take is to read more books that dig deeper into the code and building of networks that will enable you to implement in your application. You need to have a goal on how you intend to achieve this feat and even grow into this field progressively.

After you are done with this book, you will gain further understanding of the applications of Neural networks. Applications such as in fingerprint reading in cell phones and biometric systems, stock market prediction, medicine and other applications, will be a guide to understanding how you can start your applications. You will need to use this book as the foundation of the interesting world of applications.

Finally, if this book was useful in more than way, a review on Amazon will be much appreciated.

Machine Learning for Absolute Beginners

A Simple, Concise & Complete Introduction to Supervised and Unsupervised Learning Algorithms

Table of Contents

Introduction

Congratulations on downloading *Machine Learning for Absolute Beginners: A Simple, Concise & Complete Introduction to Supervised and Unsupervised Learning Algorithms*, and thank you for doing so. In the real world, companies like Amazon and Facebook and even YouTube use machine learning techniques to manage their functions efficiently. They are companies that use face recognition, speech recognition, image classification exploit k-means, deep neural networks, hidden Markov, SVM, etc. There are very many advances in machine learning that are coming up in the real world, and the applications of both supervised and unsupervised learning are growing. To get to understand what they are, you will need to get deep down into the basics, getting this book will help you have the best fundamental knowledge about machine learning.

To achieve this, the following chapters will differentiate what Supervised and Unsupervised learning are, helping you to have a better background to understand how they are used in the real world. This means that you will have to understand the analysis methods that need to come to play when you are dealing with lots of data, which is commonly defined as Big Data. The growing number of data needs to be processed with intelligent systems to bring about better solutions of the problems we are facing.

There are plenty of books that are on this subject; we are happy to help you choose this one. Every effort has been made to ensure that it is full of as much useful information as possible, please enjoy!

Chapter 1: Machine Learning Algorithm types

There is a classification that falls in machine learning algorithms which are based on the algorithm outcomes. There are several algorithm types that exist. They are listed below:

- Unsupervised learning: this involves specific inputs.

- Supervised learning: in this algorithm, there is a generation of a function that relates the output with the input. In supervised learning, the learning bit is the cause of the classification problem. The learner needs to know the function by looking at some I/O samples to map a vector into some classes.

- Semi-supervised learning - it combines the labeled and non-labeled samples to come up with a classifier or a function.

- Learning to learn: the algorithm in this type has to learn that the algorithm finds and learns the structure and bias that is dependent on the experience that happened.

- Transduction: it is quite the same as supervised learning, although it is not explicit in creating a function. Instead, it goes about to try and come up with fresh outputs that are dependent on the inputs or outputs that are being trained, and also totally new inputs.

- Learning that reinforces: the algorithm learns a new policy on how it will react when a particular observation is introduced. The impact that the algorithm has is directly felt in the environment which provides the results that help the algorithm to learn.

When you look at the performance and computations of machine learning algorithms, it is what is called computational learning theory. The topic of ML is all about the algorithmic design that makes a computer aware of the environment, adapt to it and learn it. Learning does not need to occur under a conscious structure. It only needs analysis of statistics, the regular occurrence of items, identifying patterns and predicting the next steps. This is completely different from the way a person learns something. The best part about learning algorithms is that they can provide insight into environments that are difficult to learn in a different approach.

We are currently in a historic period in our history, where computing has shifted to the cloud, from mainframes and PCs. This is not that big of a milestone, compared to what is coming in the next few years. What is even more revolutionary, are the computation tools and methods that are boosting computing. Currently, it is possible to create a complex algorithm that can crunch data for just a couple of dollars an hour.

To understand the machine learning algorithm types, you can also look at the sources below.

http://www.datasciencecentral.com/profiles/blogs/types-of-machine-learning-algorithms-in-one-picture

Chapter 2: Supervised Learning Approach

When you look at classification problems, the objective is for an algorithm or a software to learn the already created classification system. One example of a classification is how a computer learns how to recognize digits. In a general perspective, classification learning is the best approach to problems that deduce it, even though it is easy to determine the classification. There are cases where you don't have to give each instance a pre-determined classification if the responsible agent works the classification by itself. The description we have looked into is an example of unsupervised learning.

On the other hand, supervised learning normally leaves the probability for inputs not defined. If the inputs are available, there is no need to have this model. But if there are some inputs missing, it is hard to confirm the outputs. In unsupervised learning, there are variables that are responsible for the observations. This means that the results or the observations are available at the chain's end.

Supervised learning, according to training decision trees and networks, is the most common technique used. The techniques listed above rely on the provided info that is gotten from the classifications that are pre-determined. When you get to neural networks, the network error is determined by the classification used. This then leads to adjustment of the network by minimizing. In decision trees, the attributes that provide the information that is used to solve puzzles in classifications are the ones that are used in clarification.

We shall dive into this later on in the book. We are going to focus on the importance of supervision for both examples. This enables them to thrive because of their pre-determined classification.

Inductive ML is a learning process that involves a set of rules that are collected from samples. An example is a training set. It involves a classifier that generalizes relatively new instances.

Let us look at a step by step process of supervise ML.

Step1: dataset collection

When collecting a dataset, it is common also to have experts who can suggest the fields and attributes that are important. If that is not possible, then the easiest way is the brute force technique. This involves taking account of all available information, with the assumption that all features are already isolated. This type of data collection is not suitable for the process of induction since it has lots of noise and features that are missing. This makes it need a more detailed pre-processing step that is cumbersome.

Step2: data processing and data prep

There are several methods that one can choose from to be able to handle any kind of data missing. There have been researches that have identified the advantages and disadvantages of this technique. Let's look at the instant selection. It is used to cope with learning infeasibility from large data sets. An optimization problem that is instance selection tries to mine quality as it minimizes the size of another sample. Data is reduced, and data mines are maintained through an algorithm to work efficiently when exposed to big data sets.

Step3: feature subset selection

We are going to look at something that should be clear by now. The target of an algorithm that is learning is to use given inputs to minimize errors. In the problem of classification, the training set, which is the inputs, are examples which are used by the agent to enable learning. For examples, if you were going to learn XOR or exclusive OR, but you were shown one true and one false combination, but not both true or false, you will most definitely learn that the answer is true, always. The same applies to ML algorithms which involve data over-fitting and instead of learning a general classification technique, it memorizes the training set. One thing about training sets is that they don't have correct input class. If the algorithm has a powerful memory, then it can lead to problems even on special cases that do not align with the principles that are common. Overfitting is common in this instance making it hard to identify powerful algorithms that can easily learn functions that are complex to provide outputs that are general.

Chapter 3: Unsupervised Learning Approach

This is much harder than supervised learning. The main objective is to have a computer that learns how to do something that it identifies all on its own, without human intervention. There are two ways that unsupervised learning approaches this kind of learning.

First approach

This involves teaching the agent using some reward system for it to know that it has achieved the results desired. There are no explicit categorizations that exist with this approach. This training style fits well with the framework of the decision problem since the classification makes choices that take advantage of rewards and not to produce classification. The technique we have looked at comes up with agents that generalize the world, and these agents are rewarded for engaging in actions that are needful. Additionally, there is a learning approach that is reinforced in unsupervised learning. This makes the agent base their actions on rewards that occurred previously with the need of any new information, which affect the world.

If you look at it carefully, this is a pointless technique, because the algorithm will know the reward that is awaiting it, and the agent is familiar with any processing, since it is familiar with any kind of processing that is expected. It is a beneficial approach and when calculating all possibilities takes a lot of time. It is hard to learn using the trial and error approach. On a different scale, this learning style can be useful since it does not assume pre-discovered classification.

An example is the backgammon game which was defeated with computer programs that were able to learn using unsupervised learning. The programs became strong with time and outmatched the best players in chess by playing themselves several times. The principles that these programs discovered perplexed the backgammon experts. The most interesting bit is that the programs even outdid backgammon programs that were trained using examples that were pre-classified.

Clustering is another level of unsupervised learning. In this learning method, a utility function is not going to be maximized on, but it has a goal of simply finding similarities in the data that is being trained. There is an assumption that exists about the clusters matching well with the classification that is intuitive. As an example, when you cluster individuals based on demographics, you might end up classifying the wealthy, on one corner, and the poor on the other corner. Since the algorithm will not use a name for assigning the clusters, there might be a production of the names, which will then be used to assign new examples into one cluster. When data is sufficient, a data driven approach can function better. For example, filtering algorithms that are used in social information like the ones used in Amazom.com, that are used to recommend books to site visitors. These algorithms use locating principles to get similar sets, then assigning new users to them. In some instances, like in information social filtering, the cluster information on members, can produce results that are meaningful. In some cases, the clusters can be a tool used by an expert analyst. It is sad to say that unsupervised learning suffers from overfitting training data.

Unsupervised learning algorithms are made to get structure from samples of data. The structures' quality is identified by the function of the cost that infers parameters that are optimal, through minimization. These parameters characterize the structure of hidden data. The same data structures need to be provided by a second set of the source data that has been used. When there is lack of robustness, overfitting becomes the noun, from the ML literature and the statistics.

Robust learning algorithms in sample fluctuations are derived from an array of results that are deviated, and also from the learning processing max entropy principle. Unsupervised learning can be called a champion in many fields; this is testament to the world backgammon program and in driverless cars. It can develop to become more advanced when there is a discovery of a new way to assign actions and values.

When there is sufficient data, clustering comes on board, especially when there is additional data about specific cluster members, who are dependent on some data. It can also become tough at times. If the classifications are correct, classification learning becomes even more powerful. An example is the study of diseases. It is easy to come out from an autopsy, with the design of the disease; we can also have it easy when the classification is on the arbitrary thing that the computer can easily identify for us.

If we depend on the output of an algorithm as an input to some other system, then classification learning is important to that algorithm. Otherwise, it will be hard for anyone who wants to figure out the input means. As we have seen, both techniques are important and when you are choosing, figure out the circumstances of your choice. Identify the type of problem you are trying to solve, the time it needs for you to solve it, and if supervised learning is possible.

Chapter 4: Algorithm types in Supervised learning

This area is concerned mostly with classification, and there are different algorithm types that are present here. These types include:

- Linear classifiers

-Perceptron

-Naive Bayes Classifier

-Logical Regression

-Support Vector Machine

-Bayesian Networks

-Neural Networks

-K-Means Clustering

-Quadratic Classifiers

-Decision Tree which includes Random Forests

-Boosting

Let's dive deeper into these algorithm types.

Linear Classifiers

The classification goal in ML is grouping similar times in groups. These items will have the same attributes and values. It has been stated that a linear classifier uses values of a linear combination of features to make the classification decision.

If there exists a 2-classification problem, a linear classifier can be visualized operating when it is split using a hyperplane, and a high dimensional input space. When this happens, on one side resides all points of the hyperplane which is "yes", while "no" is for the rest. When there is an issue on the speed of classification, then a linear classifier is often used. This is because it is way faster. As much as this is the case, a decision tree is also faster. When the number of dimensions is large, the linear classifier also thrives in this situation. This can be seen in document classification, where the number of counts in it represents each element. This calls for regularization of each classifier.

- Support Vector machine

An SVM constructs an N-type dimensional hyper balance to perform classification. This hyper plane separates data into 2 categories, optimally. They are neural network related. To put this into perspective, a perceptron neural network has similarities to an SVM model that is using a sigmoid function.

An SVM is also closely related to the classic neural network that is a multilayer perceptron. An SVM is an option of a training method for multilayer perceptron, radial basis function, and polynomial classifiers. This occurs where the network's weight is discovered by coming up with a solution for a quadratic problem that has linear constraints. This is better than to solve an unconstrained, non- convex minimization problem, which is common or standard in neural network training.

Now, an attribute identified as a predictor-variable is used in the SVM literature, alongside a feature which is an attribute that is transformed, that define hyper-planes. With this in mind, feature selection is used to select the best representation. A vector, which is a group of features that describe a case is also used in this case. The SVM's goal is to define an optimal hyper-plane that differentiates vector clusters in a way that on one side, there are cases that have a target-variable category, and on the other side, there are cases that have the alternate category. We also have support vectors that are close to the hyper plane.

2-dimensional Example

We are going to look at an example. Let us imagine that we have a classification and we will use data that is attributed by target-variable having 2 categories. Let us also imagine that 2 predictor variables are present having continuous values. If we use the predictor's value of 1 predictor to plot a graph on X-axis and on Y-axis, you are going to see cases separation. In SVM analysis, the goal is to discover a line that splits the cases alongside their targets. The number of possible lines is numerous; the only question that poses is, "which is the best line? And how is the optimal line defined?"

When you see a dashed line laid down on parallel to the separation line of separation, it marks the separation between the nearest vector to the dividing line. The margin is the distance that lies between the dashed lines. The points or vectors that limit the margin width are what we call the support vectors.

In SVM analysis, we are going to find the oriented line so that support vectors margin is maximized. If all the analysis of s was comprised of 2 category target variables that have cluster points and 2 predictor variables was divided using a straight line, this would make the world a better place. Sadly, this is just a wish, and SVM has to deal with the following:

A) at least 2 predictor variables

B) Split the vectors that have nonlinear curves

C) Sort out cases where there cannot be cluster separation

D) Handle classifications that have more than 2 categories.

We are going to look at 3 main ML techniques and list examples on how they perform. These techniques include:

Neural Network

K-Means Clustering

Self Organized Map

K-Means Clustering

K-Means clustering guidelines that are basic are uncomplicated. We begin by defining the cluster K numbers and then assume the clusters' center. At the starting center, we are going to use any random object. Alternatively, we can also have the first K objects that are in the sequence to be the initial center. Now, with the goal of convergence in mind, the K means algorithm is going to perform three steps that are defined below.

1) Center coordinate determination

2) Distance from the center to each object

3) Based on the minimum distance, groups are created about the object.

According to some researchers, the K-Means is an unsupervised learning algorithm that is simply used to come up with solution of the clustering problem. There is a simple and easy procedure that is followed to classify any given data in clusters. The goal of these steps is to come up with k centroids of each cluster. Since different location alters the result, each centroid should be placed in a very intelligent way. The best way to achieve this is to separate them and place them in distant places from each other.

Next, you will have to take different points that belong to a set of data and find the centroid that is near, that you can associate it with. When you have no vector pending, you will have achieved the first stage where grouping occurs.

After the first stage, it is time to re-calculate the k new centroids from the previous step to come up with the clusters' bay centers. After achieving these centroids, the same dataset vectors and the newest and closest centroid will have to be bound. This will create a loop that will make it possible for us to see changes in the location of the k centroids on a step by step basis until it is not possible to create more changes.

Finally, the objective function is minimized by the algorithm, and in particular the squared error function. The steps are as follows:

1. the k points are spaced out using the clustered objects. These points are a representation of the centroids of the initial group.

2. The group that is close to the centroid is assigned an object.

3. A recalculation of the K centroid positions takes place when all objects are assigned.

4. Steps 2 & 3 are repeated until there is no more movement of the centroids. This finally brings about

separated objects that are in groups that the metric being minimized is calculated.

Although it is possible to prove that there can be termination of the procedure, the most optimal configuration is not normally found using the k means algorithm. The algorithm, by its nature, is like a child who can easily catch a cold when exposed to cold environments. This is because it is very sensitive to the cluster centers that are normally initially selected randomly. To reduce the effect we have described, the k means algorithms can be executed more than once. This is a simple algorithm that you will find in many problem domains. We shall see how it is the best solution to fuzzy featured vectors. Let us look at an example:

Let us imagine we have x samples of feature vectors s_1, s_2, $s3$..., s_n. Which are from the same class, and they are categorized in k compact clusters, k<x. Let p_i refer to the vector's mean that are in cluster i. If there is a good separation of clusters, a minimum distance classifier can be used in their separation. We now state that s is in cluster i if$||s\text{-}pi||$ is the least of all the k distances. To find the k means, follow the list:

- Initial guesses for the means s_1, s_2, s_3,..., s_n

- This is until one cannot find any more mean changes

- The estimated mean is used to create clusters of the samples

- For i to k from 1

- The mean of all samples replaces pi for cluster i

- End for

- End until

This is an easy step by step procedure which can be viewed as an algorithm that is intense in the partitioning of the x samples into k clusters to minimize the sum of the distances that have been squared, to the centers of the clusters. The weaknesses that it possesses include:

- The initial values of the means are depended on by the results produced, and suboptimal partitions are identified frequently. Different points of the start are the solution that is standard.

- The initialization way was not specified. One starting way is the random selection of k of samples.

- It is possible to find empty samples that are close to s_i, so that there is no update on s_i. This annoyance needs to be sorted in the implementation.

- The metric that is used to measure $||s-p_i||$ is depended on the results. The most common solution is the normalization of each variable through standard deviation, even though it is not a good way to go about it.

- The value of k is required for the results to be seen.

Since we never know the number of clusters that exist, it makes the last problem even tougher. Looking at the example, we have looked at above; when you apply the same algorithm to the same data, a 3-means clustering is produced. Does it mean that it is way better than 2-means clustering?

Sadly, there is no way in heaven or hell that you will find a solution that will find the number of clusters of a dataset. You can easily compare the results of the multiple executions that have occurred using different k classes, then select the best one relating to the criteria of choice.

Naive Bayes Classifier

This is a method of supervised learning as well as a method of statistical classification. This is a probabilistic model that allows for the capturing of uncertainty in the model in a manner that is principled, using the outcomes probabilities. Predictive problems and diagnostic issues can be solved by Naive Bayes classifiers (NBC). NBC was named after the famous Thomas Bayes who came up with the theorem. This algorithm provides learning algorithms that are practical. This classifier is used in the provision of understanding and evaluating several learning algorithms. Explicit probabilities are calculated to be used in the hypothesis. Its robustness is evident in the input data noise.

Naive Bayes Uses

- Bayesian Classification is a method of probabilistic learning. The classifier, Naive Bayes is one of the most well-used algorithms for the classification of text documents for learning.

- Naive Bayes is also well known in the filtering of spam emails. Spam emails are easily identified by the classifier of Naive Bayes. Apart from the modern mail clients who use the algorithm, one can also install a different filtering program. Email filters like DSPAM, Spam Bayes, ASSP and Bogofilter utilize Bayesian filtering technique and its functionality is at times placed in the software of the mail server.

- Recommender Systems that are Hybrid. Data mining and machine learning techniques are applied by recommender systems to filter information that is unseen. It can also determine if a resource can be preferred by a given user. When you combine a collaborative filtering technique with a Naive Bayes classifier, a hybrid approach that has unique switching can be achieved. When this approach was tested on different sets of data, it showed that the algorithm being tested was scalable and gave out better performance, compared to other algorithms. At the same time, it eliminates some problems that are recorded by recommender systems.

- There is an online application in the link below that has successfully modelled Naive Bayes. This application that is online is an example of a Supervised ML and computing that is affective. With the use of a training set examples that reflect nasty, nice and sentiments that are neutral, Ditto has been trained to identify each differently.

http://www.convo.co.uk/x02/

- Modelling of simple emotion takes a model that is dynamical and a classifier that is statistically based. Naive Bayes takes each word and pairs of words as features. The utterances of users are classified into nasty, neutral and nice classes with labels of -1, 0 and +1 respectively. The numerical output that is achieved takes a simple 1st order dynamical system that represents the simulation of a simulated state.

The Theory of Bayes

The reasoning of Bayes is used in making decision and statistical inferences that deal with the inference of probability. In order for it to predict events in the futures, it uses the knowledge of the past events. Let us look at an example.

Predicting colors of bricks in a box

rec	Age	Salary	Students	Loan rating	Computer purchase
R1	Equal or less than 30	High	No	Fair	No
R2	Less than	High	No	Excellent	No

	or equal to 30				
R3	31 to 40	High	No	Fair	Yes
R4	Larger than 40	Medium	No	Fair	Yes
R5	Larger than 40	Low	Yes	Fair	Yes
R6	Larger than 40	Low	Yes	Excellent	No
R7	31 to 40	Low	Yes	Excellent	Yes
R8	Less than and equal to 30	Medium	No	Fair	No
R9	Less than or equal to 30	Low	Yes	Fair	Yes
R10	Larger than 40	Medium	Yes	Fair	Yes

R11	Less than or equal to 30	Medium	Yes	Excellent	Yes
R12	31 to 40	Medium	No	Excellent	Yes
R13	31 to 40	High	Yes	Fair	Yes
R14	Larger than 40	Medium	No	Excellent	No

The Theorem of Bayes

$$P(h/D) = \frac{P(D/h)\ P(h)}{P(D)}$$

P(h) means probability that is prior to the h hypothesis

P(D) means probability that is prior to the data that is to be trained D

P(h/D) means given D finding h's Probability

P(D/h) means given h, you find probability of D

On the table above, we are going to apply the theorem

D: represents a customer who is 35 yrs. old having a $50,000 PA

H: is a hypothesis that a computer can be bought by our computer

P(h/d): Finding the probability of customer D purchasing our computer, when we know that his income and his age are correlating. (35 yrs. Old and $50,000)

P(h): finding the probability that a customer of any age (probability that is prior) purchases our computer

P(D/h): Finding the probability that a customer is 35 years old and has an income of $50,000, with an already purchased computer (probability that is posterior)

P(D): Finding the probability that one of our customers is aged 30 and has an income of $50,000

Bayesian Network

They are also known as Belief networks and they are part of the graphical models that are probabilistic. These structures represent uncertain domain knowledge. Each node represents a variable that is random, as the edges between nodes represent dependencies that are probabilistic corresponding variables, which are random. These dependencies that are conditional in the graph are estimated by the use of computational and statistical methods. Therefore, BN's merge principles from probability theory, graph theory, statistics and computer science. Undirected edge GM's are known as Markov networks or Markov random fields. These networks offer a simple independence definition between 2 nodes that are distinct based on Markov Blanket concept. In fields like computer vision and statistical physics, Markov networks are particularly popular.

BN also corresponds to directed acyclic graph (DAG) which is another structure of a GM, that is popular in machine learning, artificial intelligence, and statistical societies. BNs are what we call understandable and mathematically rigorous. An effective combination and effective representation of a probability distribution that is joint (JPD), has to be enabled over random variables.

There are two sets that define a DAG; these are set of vertices or nodes and a set of edges that are directed. The random variables are represented by the nodes, while the direct dependence is represented by the edges, which are among variables drawn using arrows located between nodes. An edge that is node X_i to X_j represents a dependence statistically between variables that are corresponding. Therefore, the arrow represents that variable X_j's value is dependent on the X_i value. X_i node becomes a parent of X_j, and X_j is referred to as a child of X_i. The acyclic graph structure ensures that no node can be its dependence or ancestor. An ancestor is a group of nodes where the node can be identified by a path that is different. On the other hand, a descendant is a group of nodes, where nodes can be identified on a path that is direct starting from the node. You should know that as much as the arrows indicate causal direct connection between variables, the process of reasoning can work on BNs by information propagation in any sort of direction.

A statement that is simple and conditionally independent is reflected by BN. Each variable is autonomous of the nondescendants if you consider the state of the parents. This property is used to minimize the no. of Parameters that characterize the JPD of variable. This brings about an effective way to calculate the probabilities of the posterior. Looking at the structure of the DAG which is normally referred to as a qualitative part, that needs to identify the parameters that are quantitative of the model. The parameters are identified in such a way that is consistent with the property of Markovian, where the distribution of the conditional property located at each node is dependent on its parents. For random variables that are discrete, a table represents the conditional probability, that lists the local probability, that feasible values are taken by a child node.

Boosting

Boosting is one of the strongest ML methods in existence today. Two of the well-known boosting algorithms, which include AdaBoost and Bagging, combine the decisions of a number of classifiers. In supervised learning, AdaBoost has been successful, but it is faced with several problems.

A) When the features are extremely large, training becomes unmanageable.

B) An imbalance exists between the negative samples and the positive samples for multiclass classification problems.

We are going to look at a 2-stage process of AdaBoost learning to select effectively, the discriminative features. Instead of boosting to occur in the original feature space, where there is high dimensionality, there will be a generation of multiple feature subspaces that have a low dimensionality. In the first stage, each subspace carries boosting. In the second stage, there is a combination of the simple fusion method and trained classifiers. When you look at the results of data that is sourced from facial expression recognition, our algorithm opposed that it can reduce the cost of training, and achieve a high classification performance.

The success that boosting algorithms have in supervised learning has extended to semi-supervised learning. The future looks bright when you look at the possibilities that come with combining boosting algorithm and graphs. This is with the intention of extending AdaBoost to semi-supervised learning and improve its performance.

The Functions of Gradient Boosting

There are 3 elements that are in gradient boosting.

a) An optimizable loss function

b) The addition of weak learners by the use of for loss function minimization

c) Making of predictions using weak learners

The Loss Function

To select a loss function solely depends on the problem in question. It has to be differentiated, but the beauty of loss functions is that many of them are able to work. There is no need to create a new-boosting algorithm for a loss function that is needed or supported; you can actually define one. For instance, squared error can be used by regression while logarithmic loss can be used by classification.

One major gradient boosting benefit is that a boosting algorithm can use a framework that is general, where a loss function uses a network that is differentiated.

The Additive Model

The addition of trees is done one at a time, while trees that exist remain unchanged. To minimize the loss in the tree addition process, one needs to use the procedure of gradient descent. The minimization of sets of parameters is done traditionally using gradient descent. The parameters that are commonly minimized include neural network weights and regression equation coefficients. After the error is calculated, or the loss is calculated, there is an update of the weights with the goal of error minimization.

Sub-models of weaker learners, like decision trees, is used instead of parameters. After the loss calculation, the addition of trees has to be done on the model that is in charge of reducing the loss, for the procedure of gradient descent to be performed. Parameterizing of the tree is the process that makes this happen. Modification of the tree parameters follows and finally, the residual loss is reduced as a sign of things flowing correctly. The general term for this process is functional gradient descent. Another alternative name functions in gradient descent.

The new tree's output is added to the existing trees sequence output to improve the model's final output. Once the loss gets to a level that is acceptable, or it stops improving on datasets that validate externally, the addition and training of a specific number of trees is done.

Weak Learner

When you look at gradient boosting, decision trees are the weak learners. Regression trees that output real values for splits, allow the addition of model outputs and the correction of predicted residuals. The creation of trees is done greedily. Basing on Gini and minimization of loss purity, the best points of splitting are selected.

When you look at AdaBoost, decision trees that are short and had one split were used. These single splits are called decision stumps, and 4-8 levels can be used in large trees. Weak learners can be constrained in some ways, like max no. of splits, leaf nodes, or layers. This ensures that there is a constant weakness in the learners, even though they can be constructed greedily.

Gradient Boosting improvements

Training data sets can be overfitted quickly by the use of a gradient boosting. Regularization methods that come from different sections of the algorithm can benefit gradient boosting, by improving the algorithms performance by the reduction of overfitting.

There are 4 gradient boosting enhancements techniques we shall be looking at.

- Tree Constraints

- Learning that is penalized

- Shrinkage

- Sampling Randomly

Tree Constraints

Weak learners possess skills even though they are weak. Constraining trees can be done in several ways. The more the number of creations of constrained trees there are, the more the number of trees that will be needed in the model, and vice versa. If there are fewer trees that are constrained, very few trees will be needed.

Here is a list of some constraints that one can impose, during the creation of decision trees.

The depth of the tree: You can say that deeper trees can be called complex trees, and shorter trees are the ones which are preferred. To get better results means using levels 4-8.

No. of trees: overfitting can be very slow when one is adding more trees in the model. What is recommended is the addition of trees until there is no improvement which can be observed.

No. of observations on each split: a constraint at its minimum is imposed on the data to be trained at the node of training, before considering a split.

No. of leaves: just like depth, no. of leaves can constraint the tree's size, but not to a structure that is symmetrical when the use of other constants is used.

Minimum loss improvement: this constraint on any slit's improvement is added to the tree.

Learning that is penalized

There can be imposition on the tree's parameters by the additional constraints, in addition to the tree's structure. CART, which is a classic decision tree, is not used as a learner that is weak; instead, a regression tree that is modified is used. This regression tree has values that are numeric in the terminal nodes, which are commonly referred to as leaf nodes. The value indicated on tree leaves can also be referred to as leaves.

The weight value of the leaves of the tree can use regularization like L1 regularization and L2 regularization to regularize.

For more details about boosting, kindly look at the sources below:

https://www.analyticsvidhya.com/blog/2015/11/quick-introduction-boosting-algorithms-machine-learning/

Neural Network

Several regression tasks can be done by neural networks. Although, each network works to handle one. In many instances, the network provides a single variable output. But in state classification problems, there might be some outputs that can be produced. The stage of post processing will handle the mapping of outputs to output variables. When multiple output variables are defined in a single network, cross talk may suffer. This means that the neurons that are hidden are going through a tough time in learning, as 2 different functions are being attempted. To come up with a better way means to use output to train the different network, and then to come up with an ensemble to run them as a single unit. The neural methods we are going to focus on include:

- Multilayer Perceptrons

It is the most popular network that is currently being used. We have looked at it briefly in other sections. Each unit performs a biased weighted sum of inputs that is passed through a transfer function for an output production. The units are placed in a feed forward kind of topology. The input output model of the network is therefore simple to interpret, with the biases and the weights of the model. Any kind of complex functions in this network can be modelled. Some of the issues that are a priority in the Multilayer Perceptron include the layers with their units, and the hidden layers. The problem defines the number of I/Os, even though the types of inputs which are going to be used is not certain. However, as of now, we shall stick with the assumption that the selection of the number of input variables is already complete. The hidden units that will be used are not clear. To start on a good point, a hidden layer needs to be used, having half the number of the I/O units.

Multilayer Perceptrons Training

After selecting the layers, units identified in the layers, the biases and the networks weight, they all have to be set to minimize the network prediction errors. This is what the **_training algorithms_** is created to do. To automatically adjust the biases and the weights, for error to be minimized, you need to gather historical cases. The process we have seen above relates to that of the networks model that presents the data available for training. One needs to run all the cases of training through the network in order to determine the error of a configuration, as you compare the real output generated with desired output. An **error function** combines the differences to provide the network error. ***Summed squared error*** which is used for problems in the regression are the most common types of the error function. They are used where the output unit's errors on individual cases are summed up, squared, and a cross entropy function is used.

In linear modeling, which is a kind of traditional modelling, using an algorithm, it is easy to determine the configuration model, to have a reduced error. A neural networks nonlinear modelling power cost is a factor that one can never be so sure about, when it comes to lowering the error, even if you can adjust the network.

Each N weights & the networks biases are considered as an N+! Network dimension error. By weight configuration, one can easily plot the error in a N+1 dimension, which forms the error-surface. The main objective of the training of the network involves getting the many-dimensional surface lowest point. In a sum-squared error functions linear model, the error surface is quadratic, meaning that the curve is smooth with one minimum. This makes to identify the minimum. Some useless features characterize the complex neural network and error surfaces. These features include a local minimum which is a lower level of the terrain, but still over the global minimum. Others include plateaus, flat plots, long ravines and saddle points.

The errors-global minimum surface is hard to determine analytically. Therefore, the neural networks training is important to explore the error surface. It starts from random weights and biases configuration, to the training algorithms which seek the global minimum incrementally. Ideally, when it comes to the creation of a move downhill, the error of the surface needs to be computed at its current position. But at a later point, the algorithm halts at a low point, which can represent the local minimum, which needs to be the global minimum.

Algorithm of back propagation

This is the best example of a training neural network algorithm. Conjugate gradient descent, which is a modern 2nd order algorithm, is faster when it comes to many problems, together with Levenberg-Marquardt. But when it comes to back propagation, it has advantages when some circumstances present themselves. This makes it the easiest algorithm anyone can comprehend.

When you look at back propagation, the calculation of the errors gradient vector is done. This vector is an idea as it looks at the slope, starting at the current point. Therefore, this makes it decrease the error when we move along a "short" distance. As the moves slow when the bottom is near, a minimum will be realized. The hard part is defining the size of each step.

When the large steps are taken, it is easy to overstep solutions or provide a wrong outcome. Looking at an example of neural network training, we can have an algorithm that continues slowly along a narrow, steep, bouncing between sides. On the contrary, tiny steps will provide the right solution, but the number of iterations needed is very many. Far from theory, the slope is proportional to the step size for the algorithm to settle at the minimum, to a special constant which is identified as a *learning rate*. When going for the learning rate, the right setting is application dependent; it may vary in time, and it gets smaller as with progression of the algorithm.

When a momentum term is included, the algorithm is often modified. The move is done in a fixed direction, so that in case some progress is made in the right way, the algorithm improves, which makes it escape the local minimum, making it move over plateaus rapidly.

The algorithm goes through **epochs** iteratively. The training cases on each epoch are submitted to the network, and the actual outputs and target are compared, and an error calculation is done. This error alongside the error surface gradient adjusts the weights, and the whole procedure is repeated. The first configuration of the network is random, and when some epoch is complete, the training stops.

Other cases that can make the training to stop include stopping of the error to improve, or in cases where it gets to a level that is acceptable. One can select which stopping condition can be used.

- Generalization and over-learning

The primary issues with this approach discussed earlier on does not belittle the focused error. This expected error that the network makes when there are identified cases will still be available. To summarize, the most appealing part of the network is the generalization of the new cases. The network is built to minimize training set error, and even if there are no perfect training sets that are large, it is not similar to error minimization that is on the surface of the error of the unknown model.

The problem of over-fitting and over-learning is an important manifestation of the distinction. A polynomial curve is the best way to show this concept, compared to neural networks, even though they share the same concept.

When you look at a polynomial, you are looking at an equation that has constant and variables. For instance, if we replace 'Y' with 'b' and 'x' with 'a', our equation would be as follows:

b=2a+3

b=3x2+4a+1

There are various shapes for polynomials that are different. They also have large numbers. When you have a data set, you may fit a polynomial curve if you want to have the data interpreted. Most of the time, the data is noisy; therefore, don't expect always to see a smooth curve or the line to go through each point. A high order polynomial is very flexible, making it possible to fit the data using a shape that is unrelated, but a low order polynomial cannot for exactly close to the points.

The same problem is shared in neural networks. A more complex function is modeled with a network with weight patterns. This makes it easy to over-fit. When you have a network that does not have lots of weights, it won't be able to create a model of the function that is present, powerfully. For instance, a network that does not have hidden layers models is a representation of a simple linear function. How will it be possible to choose the correct network complexity? A large network will get an error, but it may be tagged with an over-fitting instead of the right modelling.

The best solution is to track the progress against a data set that is independent; this is called a selection set. These cases are not used in back propagation since they are used to keep track of each algorithmic progress. Instead, it will be discovered that the networks initial performance on the selection sets, and the training is the same. Even though it may not be ideally the same, but the division cases between the sets is based. When the training is in progress, you will notice a drop on the error of the training, and with the training, it minimizes the error function that is true, and the error of selection also drops. In case the error of selection stops from declining, but rises, the network will be overfitting the data and training will stop. When the training process is in progress, and overfitting takes place, this is identified as over-learning. This now leads to a decrease in hidden layers that exist, because the network is more advanced to counter the problem in question. On the flip side, if there is a weak network, to model the underlying function, there won't be an occurrence of overlearning, and it won't matter if the selection errors or the training error drops to a level that is satisfactory.

Problems that are related to the correct network size to use and the local minima mean that a neural network involves the testing of the different network as each network is trained several times to avoid being cheated by each local maxima and to observe each performance. The selection error is the right guide to performance. If we assume that all else is equal, it is preferable to have a simple complex instead of a complex one. You can choose a smaller network instead of a large one with a slight selection error improvement.

This approach that has repeated trials has a problem. The problem is that the selection set is used to primarily select the model. This makes it part of the training process. This makes it compromise its reliability as a guide to the model's performance. When you go through various trials, you may be lucky enough to get a network that can perform well on the selection set. It is important to use a test set of data that will increase the reliability towards the model's performance at larger scale. The test data tests the final modelling in order to ensure that the outcome of the training and selection sets, are not fakes. To achieve this goal, only one use of the test data is recommended. In case this is used to alter and repeat the process of training, the data that is selected will be realized.

It is unfortunate to have divisions in multiple subsets, given that less data is normally provided than the desired amount for a subset. Resampling is the best way to counter this problem. One can conduct experiments using different data divisions into selection, training and test sets. Several ways to look the subsets are available. This includes cross validation, bootstrap, and the Monte-Carlo resampling. If design decisions are made, like the best neural network configuration to use, based on the experiments with different subset instances, there would be a more reliable result produced. That experiment can be used to help in the decision making on the type of network to use and train the networks with samples, from the beginning. This intends to do away with the bias of sampling. There can be a retaining of the networks that work well in the sampling process. When the ensemble results are looked into, there is a mitigation on the bias of the sample. Looking at the summary, after all the technical and ins and outs seen above, the network design has some of the following stages:

- First, choose an initial configuration, one that has a hidden layer with some units that are hidden which are half the sum of the I/O inputs.

- You can conduct some experiments iteratively with each configuration, using the best network. Each configuration needs a couple of experiments to counter the trickery in the discovery of a local minimum during training, and when a chance of resampling is made possible.

- If under learning happens in each experiment, this leads to the networking missing the performance level. You will then have to add to the hidden layer some neurons for a trial. If you discover that there is no change, add a hidden layer. If under learning happens in each experiment, this leads to the networking missing the performance level. You will then have to add to the layer that is hidden, some neurons for trial purposes. If there is no change, then add a hidden layer.

- When the over-learning occurs, try removing some layers and hidden units.

- Once you have determined the best networks configuration, resample and create new networks that have the same configuration.

Data Selection

The stages we have looked at assume that the training, test data, and verification must be representative of the model in question. In Neural modelling, the same idea of GIGO, Garbage in Garbage out also applies. The worth of the model relies on the training data, therefore, if it is not well represented, then it is compromised, rendering it useless. Let us look at the problems that can make the training set useless.

Training data is normally historical. But when situations change, then the past data is not relevant. It is important to make sure that all scenarios that are possible are covered. For a neural network to work well, it can only use present case. For instance, if you render employees who have incomes of $100,000 in a year as a bad risk, then if you have training data with employees who earn less than $40,000, then you should not expect the network to make the right decision when it deals with the unseen cases. It is wrong to use extrapolation when you are dealing with models, the downside in avoiding this, is that you will have neural networks that make predictions that are poor.

Easy features are learned easily by a network. To expound on this point, we are going to look at a classic example where a project that was premised with the task of identifying tanks automatically was put in place. In this project, the network in context was exposed to a 100 picture images that were not tanks, and 100 more pictures of tanks. It then achieves a score of 100%. But when test data is applied, it does not do well. What is the reason for this? The pictures which have tanks are taken when it is a rainy, dark day, while the picture which doesn't have the tanks are taken on sunny days. The differences in light intensity are what the network learns to differentiate. For it to work, the network needs cases of training on all kinds of lighting conditions and weather where it is expected to work on. You should also add pictures that have all kind of angles, terrain, and even distance.

Unbalanced data sets. It is critical to have the types of proportion data types because a network normally minimizes an overall error. If you load a network with data set that includes 900 cases that are good and 10 cases that are bad, it will make its decision with a bias to the good cases, to reduce the error. If in real proportion there is a bad representation of both the good & the bad, then the networks decision will most likely be wrong. The best example for this is on disease prevention. Now, a network is fed with training data that is on a 9 to 10 split. Later on, there are patient diagnosis that is based on complaint of a particular problem, where the tendency for the disease is on a 50 to 50 basis. The network here will fail to identify the disease in some patients who are unhealthy, because of its cautious reaction. On the contrary, if it is trained on the data complaint and a routine basis, then the network may flag quite some alerts. In these scenarios, the data set may be customized to take into consideration data distribution. For instance, you could remove some numerous cases and replicate the less numerous ones.

The best approach always has the same representation of cases that are different, and that can interpret the decision of the network.

Self Organizing Map

SOFM network is used on a different scale when you compare it to alternative networks. Since many kinds of networks work primarily for supervised learning, unsupervised learning works well with SOFM. In supervised learning, cases have both input variables that need to inference by the network, through a mapping to the associated outputs. But in unsupervised learning, there are only input variables that are contained in the training data set. It seems strange, right? What does the network use if it only has the inputs and no outputs? To answer this question like a guru, the answer is really simple, SOFM network is the answer. SOFM tries to learn the data structure.

The SOFM network learns how to recognize data clusters and relate the same classes to one another. The data that refines the network that can be understood by the user when looked at carefully. Data classes can be labelled as well as recognized, in order for the network to properly classify tasks. SOFM networks come in handy when building classifications considering that output classes which are available can be used immediately. An advantage exists, because class similarities can be brought about.

Novelty detection is the 2nd possible use of SOFM network, because, when they have a training data, they can easily learn how to recognize clusters in it and provide a response. If new data which is different from the previous cases comes fourth, the network will not be able to recognize it, and there will be novelty created.

There are 2 layers in an SOFM network. We have an input layer and also an output layer, which is known to be as a topological map layer. The output's layer units are set in space in 2 dimensions. In SOFM networks, an algorithm that is iterative is used; They start with the initial center that make up a random set, which are then changed by the algorithm to be cohesive with the clusters of training data. It compares with sub-sampling and K-means algorithm are one love, to assign SOM network centers. Indeed, the algorithm used in SOFM can be used to allocate the center of the network types. Far from that, there is another level of operation that the algorithm performs at. The network is also arranged by a training procedure that is iterative to have units representing centers that are closer in the input space, to be placed closer to the topological map. You can look at the topological layer of the network as a 2-dimensional grid that needs to be distorted and folded in the input space that is the N-dimensional, to preserve the original structure. To represent the N-dimensional space in 2 dimensions will lead to the loss of detail. However, if the technique can allow the user to visualize data, it can be worth the while, even though it can be hard to understand.

Some epochs are run by the iterative Kohonen algorithm. On each epoch, it executes every case that is used in training, to apply the algorithms as follows.

A number of epochs are run by the iterative Kohonen algorithm. On each epoch, it executes every training case and applies the algorithms as follows:

- The winning neuron which is at the input's case center to be selected

- The neuron that wins then adjusted to be the same as the input case which is a weighted sum of the training case and the old neuron center

A time decaying learning rate is used in the Algor UTN for a weighted sum to be performed to make sure that the changes are subtle when the passing of the epochs is complete. This is with the aim of having settled centers that are at a compromise, which represent cases that lead to neutron winning. If the concept of the neighborhood is added to the algorithm, then the topological ordering property is achieved. A group of neurons that surround the neuron that wins is what is called the neighborhood. It also decays over time, just like the rate of learning, for most neurons to be in the neighborhood. Later on, the neighborhood compromises only the neuron that wins. The changes of the neurons are applied to all members of the existing neighborhood and the winning neuron in Kohene algorithm.

Initially, large network areas are dragged heavily to the training cases; this is the effect of the update in the neighborhood. A crude topological ordering which is the same as cases activation clumps of neurons is developed by the network. This is done in a topological map. When the learning rate and the neighborhood are passed by the epochs, they both decrease, for finer distinctions in the map areas can be shown, which then results to neurons that are fine tuned. The following two distinct phases are conducted in training:

- A short phase that has a neighborhood and high learning rates

- Long phase that has close to zero neighborhoods and low learning rates

Once the data structure recognition is mastered by the network, it can be used to examine the data through visualization. Win frequencies can easily be checked to see if there is a formation of a unique cluster on the expected map. There is an execution of individual cases and an observation of the topological map with an intention of finding out if clusters can represent some meaning. This normally involves the use of the original application area to form a relationship between the clustered cases. When you look at the topological map, neurons are labelled for you to identify their meaning, once the identification of the clusters are done. Once the topological map is different, there can be new submissions to the network. If there is a class name labelling in the winning neuron, classification can be done. If this does not happen, then the network is rendered undecided.

SOFM are inspired by the brain's unknown properties. The brain is a large sheet of folded paper that has known topological properties, like the arm is next to the area that corresponds to the hands. SOFM is inspired by the brain's unknown properties. The brain is a large sheet of folded paper that has known topological properties like the arm is next to the area that corresponds to the hand.

Advantages and Disadvantages of SOM

Advantages of SOM

One of the best things about SOMs is that they are simple and easy to comprehend. If they are close enough, and there is connection between them, then they are similar. In case there is a disconnection between them, then they are different. Unlike N-land and Multi-dimensional scaling, they can easily be understood and used effectively.

They also work very well. They can easily classify data and evaluate the data to make sure that the quality of the calculation makes the map good as it highlights the strength of the similarities between objects.

Disadvantages of SOMs

One problem is that each SOM is different and they all find different similarities in sample vectors. Sample data is organized in SOMs for the final product samples to be similar. For instance, if you have lots of purple shades, you won't find a large group of the color in the cluster, sometimes you will get two different clusters. Just by the example of colors, we can point out the similarities between the two groups by color, but in most groups, the similarities won't be this obvious. Therefore, tons of maps will need to be developed to get one loop.

Another problem is getting the correct data. One needs to provide a value for each dimension of member samples to create a map. It is not possible to have this scenario at times, and this makes SOMs have missing data.

Finally, SOMs are normally expensive in computation. This is one major fault because the data dimensions increase, the visualization of the dimension reduction escalates to become a priority, but at the same time, the computation time increases.

Chapter 5: Comparison of Supervised and Unsupervised Learning

1. Supervised Learning

2. Unsupervised Learning

Its fundamentals are based on training data that is sampled from a data source with the right classification that is assigned. These techniques are used in MultiLayer Perceptron (MLP) models and feedforward. There are three distinct features of MLP, they include:

- Hidden layers of neurons that are separate from the I/O network layers that make the network to provide solutions to tough problems.

- There is a high connectivity in the networks interconnection level

- There is a differentiable nonlinearity in the neuronal activity

Learning through training and the features listed above provides solutions to supervised learning algorithm for error correction. This algorithm performs training to the network concerning I/O samples. It then looks for the difference between the calculated output & the desired output, and the neuron weights are adjusted dependent on the error signal's product, together with synaptic weight's out instance. Having laid out this principle, there are two faces where error back propagation learning happens.

Pass Forward

There is an introduction of the input to the network which then goes forward, coming out on the final stage as an output, after going through each step of the network.

Pass Backward

The output presented to the neuron of the output is moved backward in the network. It then calculates each neuron's local gradient in each layer and lets the synaptic weight to change concerning the delta rule.

This computation now continues for each input recursively, starting with the forward pass, then the backward pass until the network converges. Supervised learning of an Artificial Neural Network is okay since it provides solutions to nonlinear and linear possible like plant control, classification, prediction, robotics, and forecasting.

Unsupervised Learning

In SONN (Self Organized Neural Networks), learning is out carried through unsupervised learning algorithms to find patterns that are hidden in input data that is unlabeled. In unsupervised learning, it is possible to organize learned data without a signal of error to counter check on the solution. It is advantageous for the unsupervised learning when it lacks direction, because it allows for patterns to be identified by the algorithm, when it looks back on patterns that were not considered previously. Some of the major features of SOM include:

1. A signal pattern that is incoming is transformed to 1 or 2-D maps, with a target of an adaptive transformation.

2. A feedforward structure that has a single computational layer is represented by the network. The neurons in this structure are arranged in columns and rows.

3. All signals of input are stored in context to each stage.

4. Sensitive pieces of information that were related, are dealt with neurons that relate and next to each other by the use of connections that are synaptic.

Neurons compete against each other in order to be active in the competitive layer and the computational layer. Therefore, the algorithm that is used for learning is referred to as a competitive algorithm. There are three phases that Unsupervised algorithm work in SOM, this includes:

Competition phase

When the network is presented with input pattern x, the synaptic weight in the inner product is computed, and the neurons find a discriminant function in the competitive layer that motivates competition in the neurons. Close to the input vector, is the vector of the synaptic weight.

Cooperative phase

The topological neighborhood's center is determined by the winning neuron. This is achieved via lateral interaction of the neurons. Over a given period, the topological neighborhood reduces its size.

Adaptive Phase

Singular values of the discriminant function are increased on both the neighborhood & the winning neurons. This is related to the synaptic weight adjustment and the input pattern.

When the patterns in charge of training are repeated, the vectors of the synaptic weight will follow the input pattern distribution due to the neighborhood updating and the Artificial Neural Network learning, unsupervised.

In the process of classification, both learning methods group students in different characteristics. For instance, students who score high academically are categorized in a group, in another group, you will find students from less privileged backgrounds, and you will also find average students in another class.

The two results being observed are in favor of unsupervised learning since the percentage of correctness is high if you compare it with the supervised algorithm. When you look at the differences, they are not oceans apart, but with an additional layer, the correctness of the supervised algorithm can be increased. If you compare the time it takes to build a network and compare it with KSOM, it is more. Other issues that were managed by back propagation algorithm include:

Local gradient descent

By adjusting the weights, the output error is minimized by the gradient descent. The weight error change can make the error to range, leading to less reduction. This is what we call local minima. Using randomly initialized weight vectors solved this problem and when each iteration passed, the current

Network size

Problems that exist in the network size in classification that is linear, the layer that is hidden is not needed, but three classifications are needed on the error basis and on the trail to confine them in one hidden layer. The neuron selection in the layer that is hidden is another problem.

Stopping criteria

An Artificial Neural Network halts the training after it has learned the data patterns. This is done after learning mean squared error calculation is done. Sadly, the total error for the classification with four hidden neurons is 0.28 which cannot go further than that. When a trial is done to reduce the minimum, validation error increases.

Classification is an active decision-making task that is used in our academic example above. This classification might enable in allowing the students to be mentored and improve their academic performance by training and adequate attention. Additionally, it helps students to identify the lack they have on their domain and improve in that skill which benefits the students and the institution.

A classification network that is designed using some patterns is a learning observation. A new class can be assigned to a class that is existing. New knowledge and theories are facilitated by this classification in input patterns. The neural network's learning behaviors enhance the properties of the classification. We have found that algorithms used in Supervised learning, which have error back propagation are efficient for quite a number of non-linear problems that occur in real time. This can be seen in the context of the classification of students we saw. In this scenario, the unsupervised model performs efficiently when you compare it to algorithms in supervised learning.

Summary

We would like to recommend you to look at the ebook *Machine Learning for Beginners: The Definitive Guide to Neural Networks, Random Forests, and Decision Trees*. This is with the aim of getting more information and advanced in mathematical and programming knowledge of the following concepts as discussed in this book:

- Tips of Theano in Logistic regression

- A model of code on how logistic regression code is written in Theano code

- MLP as a classifier in Logistic Regression

- In-depth into Neural Networks by looking into

✓ Convolutional Neural Networks

✓ Motivation

✓ Sparse connectivity

✓ Shared weights

- Mathematical explanation of the classes of learning algorithms like

✓ Linear methods

✓ Support vector machines

✓ Neural Networks

✓ Nearest Neighbor methods

- Classification of regression trees like

✓ Tree structured models

- Mathematical foundation of Random forests

✓ Bias variance decomposition

✓ Regression

- How random forests can be interpreted

✓ Decision trees

✓ Issues that are concerned with decision trees

Conclusion

Thank you for making it through to the end of *Machine Learning for Absolute Beginners: A Simple, Concise & Complete Introduction to Supervised and Unsupervised Learning Algorithms.* Let's hope that the book was informative enough and you were able to get all the tools that you need to achieve your goals whatever it is that they may be. Finishing this book does not mean that you have all the information to help you develop something concrete in this space. You need to expand your horizons, and this will help you gain more experience and master you in the field of machine learning.

After reading this book, you will need to get practical from the theory that you have collected and brought change to the world through technological solutions to the challenges we face of processing information. There are companies that have come up with highly intelligent analytical systems that help organizations to analyze big data every day, to make business decisions. After reading this book, you now have a clue on how these complex systems come about, and you are on the forefront of being in a better place to create your system to process the kind of information you want.

Once you are done with the technical know-how on how supervised and unsupervised learning takes place, you will need to undergo a much more advanced study of the system, in order to formulate more complex systems. Finally, if you found this book useful in more than one way, a review on Amazon is much appreciated.